The Journals of
Brother Roger of Taizé

The Journals of Brother Roger of Taizé

Volume 2: 1969-1972

Brother Roger

The Lutterworth Press

THE LUTTERWORTH PRESS
P.O. Box 60
Cambridge
CB1 2NT
United Kingdom

www.lutterworth.com
publishing@lutterworth.com

Paperback ISBN: 978 0 7188 9761 1
PDF ISBN: 978 0 7188 9762 8

British Library Cataloguing in Publication Data
A record is available from the British Library

First published by Cascade Books, 2023

This edition published by The Lutterworth Press, 2024,
by arrangement with Wipf and Stock Publishers

Copyright © Ateliers et Presses de Taizé, 2023

All rights reserved. No part of this edition may be reproduced, stored electronically or in any retrieval system, or transmitted in any form or by any means, electronic, mechanical, photocopying, recording, or otherwise, without prior written permission from the Publisher (permissions@lutterworth.com).

Contents

Introduction | vii

1969 | 1
1970 | 45
1971 | 93
1972 | 127

Select Bibliography | 137
Subject Index | 139

Introduction

This book is the second in a series of volumes presenting the journals of Brother Roger, the founder of the Taizé Community in eastern France, an ecumenical community of brothers rooted in the monastic tradition. Today it numbers over eighty brothers, from over twenty-five different countries and from different Christian traditions, Reformed, Lutheran, Anglican and Catholic, who commit themselves for life to an existence made up of common prayer, work, and hospitality. Each year, tens of thousands of young and not-so-young seekers come to Taizé to spend a week of prayer and reflection in the context of a community life.

Brother Roger was born on May 12, 1915 in French-speaking Switzerland. His father, Charles Schutz, was a pastor in the Swiss Reformed Church, and his mother, Amélie Marsauche, came from a family whose roots were in France. Following his return to the faith after an adolescent religious crisis and a long bout with tuberculosis, he decided to study theology. Convinced that people needed living signs of the gospel to complement the proclamation of the Christian message, he became interested in what today are known as intentional communities.

When the Second World War broke out and the north of France was occupied by the Nazi armies, Roger felt called to leave neutral Switzerland and settle in France. He wanted to be close to the victims of the war, as well as continuing to reflect on the possible creation of a community. In August 1940 he found an abandoned house for sale in the small, isolated hamlet of Taizé, in

Burgundy, and purchased it. After the war, Taizé became the home of the community which Brother Roger founded and of which he served as prior until his tragic death on August 16, 2005 at the hand of a demented person, during evening prayer in the church.

Throughout his life, the founder of Taizé was in the habit of jotting down thoughts and reflecting on daily events in notebooks used for that purpose or on small bits of paper. Beginning in 1972, Brother Roger began publishing his diaries. The entries contained in this volume come from two books, *Que ta fête soit sans fin* (Festival without End), published in 1971, and *Lutte et contemplation* (Struggle and Contemplation), published in 1973. Since these texts were selected and sometimes written with a view to publication, they present a more continuous and accessible picture of the personal reflections of the founder of Taizé and the life of the community than the first volume, while still maintaining the freshness of a day-to-day contemplation of persons and events.

1969

In the journal entries for 1969 and the beginning of 1970, which were published in 1971 in a volume entitled Ta fête soit sans fin *(Festival without End), Brother Roger recounts the genesis of the project which was to transform significantly the life of the Taizé Community and its relationship with the young: the launching of a "Council of Youth." Two concerns of his, reflected in these pages, converged to inspire this undertaking. The first was the crisis in the Catholic Church in the wake of the Second Vatican Council, notably the many priests and religious who were abandoning their ministry. Related to this was the failure of the movement for Christian unity to achieve the results that many had hoped for after the council. At the same time, the numbers of young adults coming to Taizé and searching for a renewed society and church continued to increase, a search that ran the risk of turning into cynicism and despair if no way was found to take their aspirations seriously and orient these in a positive direction. These two themes slowly came together in the mind of the prior of Taizé, and gave rise to an ever more urgent need to take a clear and concrete step forward. This inner deliberation runs through the entries for this year, together with the ever-present reflections on nature and the community's vocation, as well as short accounts of trips to Paris, northern Italy, Switzerland, and Rome.*

February 20, 1969

When I chose the village of Taizé in 1940, I was alone. The silence of the deserts strengthens the encounter with God. Alone with ourselves, we are aware of a presence within us.

It is not consonant with our human nature to dwell in the desert. All our attention is needed if we are to come to grips with a silence that is fully alive with a presence.

For a long time our existence was characterized, not by isolation, but by an accepted solitude. And yet, from the very first day our life at Taizé has been interwoven with encounters with others. After twenty years of life together we were thrown, so to speak, into the public arena. It has taken seven years, from 1962 to 1969, for us to realize what was happening to us.[1]

While welcoming large numbers of visitors, we have always found ways of establishing zones of peace on our hill. I suspect that these simple values—silence, and also love for things, for domestic animals—strengthen a creative capacity within us.

And now, during these days, young people from forty-two countries are gathered here, quite unexpectedly, in the depth of winter. We are searching together. Forty-two countries: we are experiencing a kind of little council of youth.[2]

These young people often have a great degree of selflessness. It comes from Christ. They shun privileges for themselves, and equally they cannot stand any caste mentality. With them the church will go far.

---

1. For years only the religious press spoke periodically about the community. But in 1960 Brother Roger organized at Taizé a conference of Catholic bishops and Protestant pastors, the first meeting of this kind since the Reformation. That led to articles in *Le Monde* and *Paris-Match*, then a prime-time television program. In 1962, the Church of Reconciliation was inaugurated at Taizé, and Pope John XXIII invited two brothers to take part in the Second Vatican Council, two events that increased the community's visibility.

2. This gathering of representatives of different nations called to mind in Brother Roger the memory of the Second Vatican Council, which had ended four years previously, bringing together bishops from the entire world. He took part as an observer.

1969

February 22, 1969

Television teams in the church. The cameramen arrived without warning. What can one say? Their directors have sent them from a thousand kilometers away, one group from Rome, another from Germany. They are mostly family men. It would be inhuman simply to send them away.

I stress the need for total discretion. With high-sensitivity film they can avoid using floodlights. But I know they cannot do the impossible.

So, before the start of the common prayer, I am obliged to take the microphone and to explain once again to those present: "Today during our prayer, cameras will be on us for a few minutes. Some of us, because we take prayer so seriously, will find this intrusion hard to accept. There are others, just as serious, who are glad of the possibility of communicating with large numbers of people."

February 23, 1969

A long talk with a brother. He questions me about the prayer I improvise each day in the church at midday. He asks why, in it, I allude so often to darkness, to inner poverty, to night. Because I do not base my life on illusions. I am aware of the combat being waged within the Body of Christ, the church. Certainly the church will emerge from this combat: she does not die. Continually in a state of being born, she is created ever anew.

As for our own dark nights and poverty, I can talk with God about them all the more readily since, at present, so many Christians are aware of their limits. Personally, I have no need to conceal my poverty. There, I contradict those who suppose that our vocation confers some kind of privilege. Like them, with them, I set out daily on the same road, out of my night towards a light—or even from doubt towards believing.

February 24, 1969

Do not confuse being emotional with being sensitive. I refuse to be emotional (not the same thing as having rare, deep emotions): I have better use to make of my energies—they are already none too great. I refuse to be emotional since my progress—like that of our community, of the church or of whole societies—does not at all depend on that. Whereas sensitivity remains alive in many grave situations.

February 26, 1969

Robert Kennedy tells somewhere how difficult it was for those who met his brother, the president, to be themselves. Each visitor tended to enter into what he sensed of the president's line of thinking. One day, going with a friend to see his brother, he was astonished to hear his friend expressing the opposite of what he had determined to insist on. How can highly placed statesmen be kept informed?

And it is the same in the life of the church. More than once I have been known to ask my brothers, before some conversation, to pray for me to remain myself and to keep my courage.

February 27, 1969

In the next world we shall be astonished to meet those who, unacquainted with Christ, have lived by him without realizing it.

March 1, 1969

Several times in recent years, I have heard Protestants (some of them pastors with personal positions of authority) repeat: "Since the Vatican Council, the Catholic Church has replied to the questions posed by the Reformation to such an extent that Protestantism has lost its reasons for existing apart; all its best aspirations are henceforth embodied in the Catholic Church. Are we now going to act in consequence, or are we going to invent new reasons to justify being separated?"

And today the question arises: is protest not taking over now within the Catholic Church itself? I should never have thought so, even a few years ago. The Reformation of the sixteenth century sought to protest against abuses and to that, answer has been given. Today, within the Catholic Church, protesting does not necessarily have abuses as its target—at times it becomes an end in itself. Almost everything is called into question. We are far from the point at which ecumenism began. A great storm has blown and, at moments of calm, we look around wide-eyed to see what has held firm.

March 2, 1969

Little Bruno baptized in the village church at Taizé. His parents are not involved in the life of the parish and so the priest had asked them to put off the baptism until later. But when he saw their stupefaction and their real desire to understand, he finally agreed.

And what a festival! Obvious astonishment on the part of the family. The grandfather is unable to recognize anything from previous occasions. He finds everything easy to grasp, accessible. "It's because of the Council," I explain. And a few days later he is heard to say, "Everything has totally changed; it's because of the consul."[3]

Back from the baptism, a brother tells me that a local man, the young father of a family, has just died. I remain silent in my room. I was almost unacquainted with that man, who spent all his holidays in his family home near Taizé. His family held in conscience that no contact between us was possible for doctrinal reasons. Four years ago, on the morning marking the twenty-fifth anniversary of my first arrival in Taizé, I went to a Mass celebrated by a priest

---

3. *Translators' note:* The grandfather's misapprehension is not so unnatural in French, since the word *concile*, used for the ecumenical councils of the Church, is a rarity, quite distinct from *conseil*, the word for a council in the everyday sense.

of the same family—a true patriarch in the midst of his people. I had let it be known that I would be there. The Mass over, everyone left and I remained alone, waiting for the priest to come out of the sacristy. Not seeing him come, I ventured to go and greet him. His welcome was, "The church is intransigent." "True," I replied, "yet everywhere openings are being prepared." And I attempted to explain all that we are involved in with Catholics—those of Latin America, for example.

March 4, 1969

This morning a letter from the widow arrived. Replying to a message I had sent, she writes, "The assurance of the prayers of your community reached me at the very moment that the Lord called my husband to Himself. . . . And since I have the opportunity today, I want to tell you how, although we never had the joy of talking with you, your thoughts have often been the source of our reflections as a couple—perhaps particularly *Living Today for God*, which we frequently read and meditated on together."

Already, beyond the divisions, there had been a contact. I am overwhelmed.

March 5, 1969

Among Christians and atheists alike, too much vital energy is used up in constructing abstract, ideal forms of society; at the end of it all lots of ideas, but nothing is really achieved for humanity. Protest itself is now becoming another ideology, instead of being creative criticism.

I can see nothing more appalling than to live as an ideologist. Seek to free myself from ideologies—refuse the luxury of wasting the energies so vital if the earth is to be made a place fit to live in.

1969

March 6, 1969

Alternation, the provisional—two values I believe in profoundly! But I know too that for some people they serve to disguise a basic dissatisfaction. As though change can have magical results. True, a change of scene can give a person a momentary sense of peace which distracts them to such an extent that they may believe they have already been transformed. But time goes by, and the day comes when they find themselves once more confronted with themselves. Inwardly, in spite of the uprooting, nothing is really different. And there they are, insatiable once again. Let's make a change—so I can stay as I am. Let's make a change, then I shall not have to pay the price of a personal transformation. And the cycle begins anew.

March 7, 1969

Who can seize all that a look conveys? I listen to a brother. One word painstakingly follows another. If there were only the words, I should be unable to understand completely. But in his eyes there shines a struggle—the refusal to serve himself at another's expense.

March 8, 1969

What can Christians do to promote development? Above all, help make people—and especially Christians—more aware of the injustice and inequalities in the distribution of wealth. Generation after generation, in season and out of season, reawaken the hardened conscience of our societies.

We know that what we do remains symbolic. Only nations have sufficient means to change the situation. If at present they are shunning their responsibilities, it is up to us to make up for them temporarily.

March 9, 1969

Dryness in the personal encounter with Christ. Nothing seems to be happening. The days go by; time runs on. Even the value of the searching only appears later. It is certainly not to be more at ease in oneself that one perseveres in this faithfulness. What is at stake lies elsewhere and is far greater.

Community prayer too has its deserts to cross. But it is lived out with many others. We see faces and it overflows into a celebration of friendship.

March 16, 1969

Sunday morning in Paris with my mother, my sisters, and their children who have come to visit us. A brother celebrated the Eucharist. The day's reading was the multiplication of the loaves and fishes.[4] Ever since my early childhood I have experienced the reality of this text. My mother used to assure me that we would always have enough to fill us, and much, much more. As a tiny child, I used to long for there to be an organ in the parish church. To which she would reply, "One day you will have one."

After the Eucharist, I am reluctant to go out to Mass. I should be sure to meet many friends there. I should want to invite them, and I have very few days of holiday with my mother and sisters.

Now my sisters have gone out, to Mass or to Sunday worship. Everything breathes peace. Peace resting in the light that every now and then floods the white pages I am covering with the thick strokes that compose my writing.

Hanging on the wall of my room is a Catalan Christ, with the four evangelists at his right hand. His outstretched hand blesses us by night and by day. Green golds predominate. The artist can have had nothing but gold and pale green on his palette.

All the doors have been left open. In every room someone is writing. At the far end, my mother is installed. At eighty-nine, she still works every morning on her correspondence. In the room

4. John 6:1–15.

next to hers is the oldest of all my nieces. In the dining room a brother has taken a seat at the big table, also to write. I go to the record player to play Pergolesi's *Stabat Mater* once again.

March 17, 1969

Went shopping in the department store in the Rue de Rennes. Going down to the toy counter, I ask what inexpensive items they have for children. Timidly the salesgirl tells me, "Father, last Sunday I heard you speak on the midday news, talking about Latin America. And I told my husband, 'I know him; Father comes to my counter.'" She sells me eighteen dolls, reduced in price, and eagerly runs off to look for other toys in the stock.

Not content with that, she asks her colleagues to look and see if they have other things that do not cost very much.

Opposite the toys is the jewelry counter. The salesgirl there, a colored girl, tells me, "Keep my counter for me for a moment, while I go and see one of my co-workers who's bound to have something for you."

March 23, 1969

Back in Taizé, I learn of the death of a Portuguese immigrant at Cormatin.[5] He leaves behind eight children, some still infants. This afternoon at their house, the oldest son told me of his father's last hours. Struck down by a hemorrhage, he insists on seeing the priest to confess, be anointed, and receive communion. Then, for the last three days, he comforts his family and reassures everyone coming to see him that they will all meet again, with Christ. He keeps a picture of the Virgin of Fatima before him.[6] He keeps kiss-

---

5. A village four kilometers from Taizé in the direction of Chalon-sur-Saone.

6. In 1917, during World War I, three poor shepherd children in the town of Fatima, Portugal, reported six apparitions of the Virgin Mary. The reports were very controversial, partly for political reasons, but the location attracted many pilgrims, and the Catholic Church officially recognized the apparitions in 1930. Today Fatima is an important place of pilgrimage and has been visited by recent popes.

ing the image and saying, "The Virgin is here." His last words are for her. Sometimes he weeps, but never when his wife is there.

This afternoon we told each other how this death can only bring us closer together. Before parting, we kneel down. First, the mother makes her children kiss the picture of the Virgin, then she prays in Portuguese. The two smallest ones do not know how to make the sign of the cross; she asks them to repeat the words of the prayer again, pronouncing them better.

At home, I tell my brothers of the visit. I ask: "In spite of the subsequent political uses made of it, why should not the mother of Christ have appeared to three children of Fatima to comfort the poor of a people who were to suffer so much. What does it matter if the image described by the children is not to our taste? Any apparition is always impossible to translate into pictures."

April 2, 1969

Talk with five seminarians. They manifest a collective anxiety. I attempt to fix their minds on the essence of the church's life; they listen attentively. They are eager for something, but what exactly? What will become of them? Will they have a share in building up Christ's body, or in breaking it down?

Next, among others, is an old couple. Their mutual love is so genuine. She is silent, but her eyes convey a friendship with God.

Here, at the same spot, not long ago I received a young widower. And today I learn that he has taken his life. Why did I not realize then that it would come to that? When I saw him, he had just lost his wife and nothing could console him.... I tried to reassure him, but all I could see were two wide eyes flooded with tears. I insisted that he should not remain alone for the moment; he had children to live for. I was ready to take any steps to help him—to welcome them here for a while.

1969

April 8, 1969

Earlier this year, we began singing a short Gregorian hymn in Latin at Sunday evening compline.[7] Today the question was: "But whatever for, when you are not obliged to use Latin?" My reply: "Because we are free men. In singing that age-old hymn, we are being nonconformists."

April 9, 1969

Trials are with us, palpably. In the past they would have brought me down, for a moment, by their sheer dead weight. But this evening I found myself telling a brother, "I am a man blessed beyond measure." By what am I blessed? By our monastic calling, by the love of my brothers.

April 10, 1969

In our old societies, there is enormous scope for neutralizing each other. Behavior is dominated by the fear of dangers. Little springtime sap in a civilization that has reached its autumn. Fewer new bursts forward that endure. Our spontaneities rarely know a second morning.

April 11, 1969

Three cows have just arrived at the house—we had previously given them all to the cooperative farm.[8] With them here, we shall have a direct presence of one quality of rural life—the cycle of the seasons. In late autumn the three cows will settle in the stable; sly

---

7. Night prayer.

8. In 1962, in the wake of Pope John XXIII's encyclical *Mater et magistra*, five farmers in the area, together with the community, combined their farms to start a cooperative, the COPEX. One of the brothers, Alain Giscard (1929–), worked there full-time until his retirement.

visits late at night, when everything in the stalls breathes calm and warmth of welcome.

April 13, 1969

Once again, a youth asks what prayer can be for him. To begin with, I tell him, "Do not look for a solution that fails to take your humanity into account. Personally, without my body I should have no idea of how to pray. I am no angel and I have no complaint about that. At certain times I sense that I pray more with my body than with my understanding. Such prayer is at ground level—on one's knees, or bowed down, looking towards the place where the Eucharist is celebrated, taking advantage of the peaceful silence and even of the sounds coming up from the village. The body is really and truly present to listen, understand, love. It would be sheer folly to want to leave it out of account!"

April 20, 1969

Longing for spring to arrive: the cold weather persists but the brilliance of the garden gains by it. For three weeks now gold has been singing in the daffodils, red in the tulips. The chill in the air keeps them from wilting.

At this time of the year I am always transported in my innermost heart. I want to miss nothing of the laboring of the plants and trees, so I set my table close against the high window filled with daylight from the north. Then I carry my papers to the desk near the window that opens directly to the south. A disturbance in the air: already the first squeaks of the lightly shaken shutters announce an approaching squall; it comes, great drops whipping the southern panes. I return to the north. There, all is peace and serenity. A misty curtain, the rain driven in successive waves, is mounting the valley from the south.

On the rare occasions when I have chanced to be in town at this season, the springtime struck me as less glorious, but there was the same cheerful gladness. Even in town, I watch for signs: a bud, sheltered by a high facade, bursting open before many others; the morning light; the freshly lit clouds chasing by, high above the roofs.

April 21, 1969

Progressive or conservative, the two attitudes may well spring from one and the same source and have a regression as their motivation. For the progressive, a regression towards adolescence, the age when things break apart, when all continuity is seen as a restraint. For the conservative, regression towards a far distant past, lying before birth—nothing can be sound unless it belongs to that period.

April 22, 1969

Living close to the earth, I need the city. There, human creation lies at every turning. The imagination is awake to grasp the way in which the relationships of a multitude are harmonized.

Living close to the earth, conscious of the limitations that result from this sometimes excessive love for creation, I need—if I am to understand other people—to listen to those who are poles apart from myself. All of us, whether we know it or not, are penetrated by the waves of contemporary thinking. Rather than remain unaware, I want to understand, and here on the hill I am granted moments when I listen to people pursuing research in various fields: theology, computer science, psychoanalysis, Marxism....

Living close to the earth yet friend of the great cities, unanimity is built up painstakingly within me, when I am in our church together with my brothers and many others.

April 23, 1969

In the Southern languages the word for church means gathering or, even better, assembly: *ecclesia, église, iglesia, chiesa*. In the Northern languages the church is designated by the name of the Lord (*Kyrios*): *church, Kirche, kyrka, kerk*. So here too South and North complement one another.

May 7, 1969

The body can only move by obeying the feet—and they only go ahead one at a time. If we hurry too much, we only get out of breath! All the excess work, all the letters waiting to be answered are nothing to be upset over. One step after another, one job at the end of another.

May 8, 1969

The burden resulting from so many people giving up and fleeing the church is practically overwhelming. How unfathomable is unfaithfulness. My life has been harrowed by it. At these points Christ awaits us, in agony for every human being.

May 9, 1969

When our imagination spends time dreaming up projects for the future of those entrusted to us, it may prevent us from grasping, at the right moment, the will of God.

And at the same time imagination, as a creative force, drives us out of ourselves and enables us to seek some change, some transformation, for other people.

1969

May 10, 1969

It is good to write each day and if necessary to oblige myself to do so. It is my handiwork, as someone else pounds dough and bakes bread. It is the means of a fundamental independence.

May 12, 1969

Heat invades the hill; at dawn I went to the narrow bathroom window to view the mist-bathed garden; I lay down again; on reawakening, summer had burst out.

When I was a child, I would make my song of this May 12. From top to bottom of the house I used to thunder, "Today's my birthday, the best day of the year!" Out in the garden, I would go to see if a peony had opened during the night. I used to encourage it by forcing apart the protective petals to set free the crown.

This morning, as in the past, I went to look at the peonies. They were still shut.

On the way back from morning prayer, brilliant sunlight was bathing the oak standing at the bend in the path between the church and the house—we call it the "oak of Mamre."[9] I was surrounded by brothers laughing to see my enthusiasm at living this day, when I am fifty-four years old.

A thought crosses my mind: today will go without a hitch. In the mail, nothing difficult; among the birthday greetings, a letter that I had confidently been expecting for a long while; suddenly, a telephone call from outside. The call goes on and on; will it never end? A jolt for this day: I had so wished to live it peacefully.

This evening, another telephone call, from Chicago: warm, joyful voices, my brothers. . . .[10]

---

9. In the Bible, Abraham's tent was located near the oaks of Mamre (Gen 18:1).

10. After the Second World War, when life in Taizé became less arduous, brothers were sent out across the world in small groups, known as *fraternités*, to live in places of poverty and division, "to be a sign of [Christ's] presence among all people and bearers of joy" (Brother Roger, *Rule of Taizé*, 95). From 1966 to 1972, some brothers were living in a poor neighborhood of Chicago.

May 20, 1969

The refusal of efficiency becomes an efficacious sign that corresponds so well to the needs of humanity.

May 24, 1969

At the present time, I often go to the small village church, close to the reserved Sacrament. There is a presence there, witnessed to by the faith of the Catholic Church since the first centuries.

Why do I never go to pray before the reserve of eucharistic bread conserved after the Lord's Supper? Could it be that the faith of the non-Catholic churches has not found itself confirmed there by the custom of centuries?

May 30, 1969

Everyone is marked for life by the encounters of their earliest years. When I was five, I spent one Sunday with my sisters in the region of Estavayer.[11] Late in the afternoon, on the way back to the waterfront from which we would cross the lake, we went into a Catholic church. Everything was veiled in shadows. The light shining before the Virgin and the eucharistic reserve has remained an unaltered image in me.

A few years later I went to Besançon[12] with my parents to visit an uncle. Opposite the house lay a church. I shall never know why, but one morning, I rose before any of the others, and went into the church where Mass was being celebrated. On my return I found the family breakfasting. They were all surprised that I had gone out so early and it was hard for me to say where I had been, because of my uncle, as though I had somehow compromised him.

---

11. A small town located in front of Provence, Brother Roger's birthplace, on the other side of the Lake of Neuchatel. As part of the canton of Fribourg, its population is mainly Catholic.

12. A city in eastern France, close to the Jura mountains and the border with Switzerland.

June 6, 1969

To set one's own self forward leads invariably to hopelessness.

In my personal life, marked by Christians unable to understand our vocation at Taizé, it takes all my vigilance not to look for compensations. Like blame, praise poisons. It stimulates for a moment, when one has been humiliated by seeing one's intentions distorted. But one hurt is scarcely soothed before we come to desire more praise. Courting criticism would be of no help, as though the harshness of judgments would cure us of the need to be reassured. Blame simply leaves us in doubt and confusion.

June 9, 1969

A few weeks ago, a German television channel asked to interview me in my room. And the first question began, "You who are Protestant..."

Spontaneously, an unexpected reply burst out: being Protestant has meant, for over four centuries now, protesting against the Catholic Church. But I do not protest against her. If I sometimes express a refusal, it is just as much against certain Protestant attitudes as against Catholic ones.

What an idea to program one's life on protest!

June 11, 1969

Before waking, a dream: someone invisible lays a figure of Christ in my hands. I speak a word of happiness, I forget just what. . . . Christ very close to me: that's all, I am not interested in knowing anything more.

June 12, 1969

This morning a Jesuit asked me: you say you wish to see the ecumenical vocation lived out, rather than talked about. Are you then opposed to research on doctrinal questions? My reply: several times each day we pray the liturgy—the prayer of the church of all ages—and gradually we absorb the great themes of the faith; theology soaks into us. Without that prayer, we would never have sung and lived the resurrection to such an extent. The celebration of Christ comes first, but the need to express it in theological language follows naturally, as a direct consequence.

Besides, theology is surely also situated in an intimate relationship with God. If it is knowledge without contemplation, it loses all its creativity. What is harsher than someone whose theological scholarship is not flooded by the freshness of communion with an Other?

June 13, 1969

For months now, one thing has been preoccupying me: with the present discord in the church, what act could give peace to those who are shaken and strength to those who are committed?

I sense that such an act should be a gathering of a demanding nature, regularly repeated for years to come. Over a certain period of time, building and searching together. And with that, again and again the same thought dominates: this demanding gathering is going to be a council of youth. But who will carry it out? As far as we are concerned, there is no comparison between the effort required and our possibilities.

Besides, if we set out in that direction, what trials lie in store for us! Oppositions are bound to arise, whereas peace and friendship are priceless values. Where to find new courage?

June 24, 1969

With four of my brothers, two days spent visiting the bishop of Crema in northern Italy.[13] My room is high in the bishop's house.

---

13. Carlo Manziana (1902–1997), a priest of the Oratory of St. Philip Neri in Brescia, was a childhood friend of Giovanni Battista Montini, the future

1969

This morning, from my bed, my eyes could not tear themselves away from the Lombardic frieze running around the cathedral. To think that I am here, in the home of such a genuine witness! From my window, waiting for it to be time for Mass, I could look down on the two sisters on a lower floor, coming and going with hushed steps, opening shutters, watering the flowers on the terrace, replacing a faded geranium with a fresh one. I had to wait for the bishop, always an early riser, to awake. He had stayed up too late last night because of us. At last, his shutters swung open.

Meanwhile, I strolled as far as a hidden door leading on to the terrace. Behind it, buried in the thickness of the cathedral wall, lay a tiny loggia opening into the church. The sanctuary was bathed in pale gold. In the presence of an early morning congregation, priests were celebrating Mass according to the new texts.[14] In their gestures, their movement—first to the lectern, then from the lectern to the altar—I beheld an unexpected dance: David's joy before the ark.[15]

June 25, 1969

We pursued yesterday's conversations with the bishop. I was eager for him to realize one thing: all that I came to confide to him, to hear his opinion on, is likely to lead my brothers and myself to new commitments. After so many years of struggle, I appreciate the peace and quiet of the last few months. Shall I have the courage to undertake a daring new venture for Christ and his church?

Pope Paul VI. For his antifascist leanings he spent fourteen months in the concentration camp at Dachau during World War II. Named to the small diocese of Crema by Paul VI in 1963, he applied the teachings of the Second Vatican Council there with conviction. Brother Roger made his acquaintance at the Council, and they became good friends, which is why Brother Roger went to consult him concerning the project of a "council of youth." He was sometimes asked to explain informally to the pope certain initiatives of Taizé.

14. The renewed liturgical texts that were one of the achievements of the Second Vatican Council.

15. See 2 Sam 6:12–15.

Upon awakening this morning, I realized that I was afraid. Where to find the courage?

Two hours after our final conversation, the five of us were at Sotto-il-Monte, the home village of John XXIII. When we arrived at the Roncallis' house we see, standing in front of the gate in the yard, the old peasant Zaverio Roncalli. He has an astonishing resemblance to his brother, Pope John.[16] I met him once before, but he appears not to remember. Talking with us, he pronounces a word, *"Coraggio!"* and adds, in his rugged dialect, *"Sempre avanti"* (ever onwards).

We go to the parish church, where his brother was baptized. We sing some psalms, an alleluia, and stay for a while in these haunts of a childhood. As we are about to leave we agree, with one accord, that we want to see Zaverio Roncalli's house once again. He is still at the same spot. I remind him of his two expressions. He asks who is driving and says, "He drives, you bless." And then he adds, raising a finger, *"Sempre Spirito"* (always the Spirit), and these last words, *"Mai paura"* (never fear).

We had not come to ask him for anything. The man who spoke those words is poor, and very old. He cannot know what he gives with a few syllables. We may never know the best that we have to live for others, and perhaps it is better that way.

July 2, 1969

Burning heat, banished tonight by a strong wind. The windows and shutters have begun to rattle. It is one in the morning.

All around the house, a flood of cool air. A perfumed breeze infiltrates my room, hitherto scorchingly hot, and brings repose. There was no hint of this sudden change coming. This evening, towards the west, enormous white clouds fringed with gold were towering into the sky.

Sunsets fascinate me, whatever the season. Enraptured, I could stand watching them for endless hours. My dream is to have

---

16. Pope John's baptismal name was Angelo Giuseppe Roncalli.

a window giving on to a vast western horizon. Filled by all that the day had brought, I could remain alone before these signs of the infinite without even noticing my solitude.

This year I often seek out, late in the evening, the glow that is still visible to the north in the distant darkness. And rising with the dawn I hasten into the garden, better to realize the shortness of the night.

Awaiting the day! In the present convulsions of society, certain persons already sense the splendor of the coming day. Only things ardently longed for take on a great capacity for joy.

July 3, 1969

Concerned this morning to find someone to write a text about Taizé. The time limit is expiring. If we do not choose someone ourselves, the publishers will commission a writer, and perhaps he will be unable to understand us.

A name comes to mind: Jean Vivien.[17] But how to contact him quickly? Besides, a heart attack brought him just recently to the very edge of the grave.

Then, this afternoon, I learn that Jean Vivien just happens to be passing through Taizé. I can scarcely believe it. I tell him what is bothering me. Without hesitation he agrees to write for us. We understand each other just as well now as on the first day we met.

July 5, 1969

I have been to see a brother on his hospital bed. Why does he have to undergo these repeated trials? The burns on his face mask that look of limpidity that has ever been for me an invitation to openness, all through the seventeen years that he has been a brother.

---

17. Jean Vivien, a pastor from Neuchatel, Switzerland who was a close friend of the community.

July 6, 1969

Yesterday at Macon, going to buy some thermometers in a shop where I had never set foot before, the salesman asked me if it was from Taizé. But how could he know where I come from? In the car, I asked Patrick[18] about it. He assures me that it frequently happens, in different stores in Macon. We must all have a family likeness, built up bit by bit. This is true for all those who have to sustain a single combat together and who remain attentive to one another.

July 7, 1969

This morning a card arrived announcing the death of Marie Braillard, at the age of eighty-four. I knew her when I was young. Only a few days ago, I was in Switzerland with some of the brothers and we decided in the spur of the moment to make a detour by way of Chapelle-sur-Oron.[19] There I entered the farm of the Braillard family—the last time I was there was at least fifteen years ago. I found Marie Braillard sitting in the kitchen talking. She recognized me at once. Taking my hands she said, "Roger, you are here—and I had been asking that I might see you again before I die. Just the other day the radio said that you were at Geneva for our Pope's visit and that made me happy. My niece has always been too shy to write to you, but we often talk about you." And five days later, she died.

---

18. Brother Patrick (Robert Stahl, 1926–), a French brother who often served as Brother Roger's driver in those years, as well as working in the garage of the community and in the printing workshop.

19. A village in the Catholic Swiss canton of Fribourg, very close to the town of Oron-la-Ville, in the largely Protestant canton of Vaud; Brother Roger's father was pastor there for some time. Brother Roger took long walks in that region while recovering from tuberculosis as a teenager.

July 14, 1969

Fine weather has set in once again. The birds are silent, overwhelmed by the heat. Two skylarks, high in the sky, cry their clear song.

July 16, 1969

Yet another Catholic exhorts me to free Taizé of all reference to the hierarchical church. For him it is doomed; it means nothing to people today; by our desire to maintain a communion with it, we are tying our own hands.

I have nothing to reply. Of course, I too wonder how authority will be exercised in the church in the future. After being identified, in every church, with juridical and temporal power, after relying for support on political power to such an extent, how is authority now going to right itself vigorously enough for it to make clear that its driving force comes from elsewhere? With the passing of time, most—not to say all—of the Reformation churches have fallen into this same trap. But I also know that at present the hierarchy is purifying itself. It could not simply disappear, or the whole body would promptly fall apart—of that I am convinced.

July 20, 1969

Twenty-five years ago today, the failed attempt on Hitler's life.[20] In that particular case, destructive violence—killing one man—would have set millions free. We would have been spared those last ten months of war, when atrocities multiplied so appallingly in the concentration camps and in the occupied lands. And the massacre of the German resistance families would also have been avoided.

---

20. In 1944, some high-ranking German political leaders and senior military officials hatched a plot to assassinate Adolf Hitler, known as Operation Valkyrie, in the hope that they could then negotiate an advantageous peace settlement with the Allies. The attempt misfired, and the conspirators were all sentenced to death.

Today two men will reach the moon. A certain line of research had as its first results the destruction of whole cities. Since then, the same scientists have been preparing a new dawn, full of promise.

July 30, 1969

Rediscovery of the mildness and peace of certain late afternoons that announce the coming autumn. Fulfillment. Nothing more desirable than the stone bench at the west corner of the garden belonging to my sister Genevieve.[21] Time stands still.

I asked some young monks from St. Benoît-sur-Loire[22] this question: desacralization may be at its height, but are we not effecting a resacralization without realizing it? Sacralizing all that is instantaneous or provisional. I may have contributed to this movement, partly by publishing *Dynamic of the Provisional*—so I am told, and I am prepared to believe it. But I regret nothing. In that book I tried, it is true, to express the present aspirations towards spontaneity at a time when they could only just be sensed, but at the same time setting them in close complementarity with the continuities of a whole lifetime.

While writing these lines, I hear a blackbird spinning out his song. His creation enchants both of us.

July 31, 1969

Tiredness since rising. Could I have forgotten the sources of refreshment? Entrusting cares and opponents to God sets free new energy; it enables us to look beyond situations, and beyond

---

21. Genevieve Schutz (1912–2007), Brother Roger's youngest sister, joined him in Taizé during World War II to help with the welcome of refugees. After the war, she acted as a mother for twenty boys orphaned by the war and raised by the community. She never married, and lived in Taizé for the rest of her life, having given up a promising career as a concert pianist.

22. An important Benedictine abbey in central France, founded around 630.

persons. Perhaps in this way we already get in touch with a portion of eternity.

August 1, 1969

A young Venezuelan was saying at table today how, in the early centuries of the church, Christians regarded heresy above all as a lack of charity, not as wandering away from orthodox belief.

August 5, 1969

Night of the Transfiguration. Festival of the present age. Our century has discovered depths in humanity so vast that we sum up within ourselves the whole of humanity, from its origins until now. But to these vast spaces underlying the human person is offered a transfiguration.

August 9, 1969

Letter from the aged aunt of a brother. She had heard a broadcast recorded at Taizé and, from the farm in the Jura mountains where she lives alone, she writes, "In this agitated world there is a secret movement, visible here and there. Let us go forward."

August 10, 1969

A new tendency is becoming clear among the thousands of young people who have stayed at Taizé this year. A few years ago, it would have been usual for them to oppose any man who, in their eyes, represented authority. The great wish was for the death of church institutions. This year the search for Christ predominates.

Yet this morning I was constantly under attack—not by young laypeople but by religious and priests. The Divider has kept back a choice zone of action for himself. He is hard at work at the heart of the church, among those who have consented to exercise a ministry for their entire lifetime. Originally, many of them were of a will to purify the church. That has now changed into hostility, or sometimes hatred.

I can only repeat the same words: by despising the church, you are destroying yourselves—you are members of the body of Jesus Christ. But they seem to have made their choice.

August 11, 1969

Tonight we should have seen the largest number of shooting stars. But the sky is overcast. We had forgotten what it was like, after four weeks of hot weather, with the host of stars sheltering the hill beneath a vast, spangled cloak.

August 13, 1969

Surely the Catholic Church, throughout her history, being the *catholica*, after the failures when she turns in on herself, constantly seeks ways of being a place of communion for the multitudes? If present trials make her more fragile, they also cause her to become more permeable. I have confidence in her because, in spite of all the inertia, she has offered the means of living by the two promises of Christ: "This is my body"[23] and "Whatever you unbind on earth will be unbound in heaven."[24]

August 14, 1969

On my writing table, a bouquet of purple and orange flowers, crowned by three sunflowers. A background of ivy supports the different strands of the polyphony. I cannot concentrate on the blank page; irresistibly my eyes lift and my heart overflows.

---

23. Matt 26:26.
24. Matt 18:18.

One of the letters in this morning's mail was from Olivier.[25] To read it fills me with happiness. I simply cannot believe it was meant for me: "I have not stopped thinking about you and our conversation before I left. You are ever the brother I would want. . . . All the things that unite us, these last seventeen years, fill my heart and help me discern God's will in spite of life's contradictions. With you I advance from my night towards the light of Christ."

August 15, 1969

Last night's prayer, at three in the morning, was utterly simple. At our midday meal, I asked my brothers the question of their being a prayer every night, ensured by a few of us. Then if someone awakens in the night, he could have the delight of joining his brothers in the church.

It is almost seven in the evening. I am writing with my window open towards the blue line of the distant heights that drop down towards the Chalonnais. The fountain is uttering the same note as in the middle of last night.

August 16, 1969

The weight of all the battles to be waged! I consent to fight—there is beauty even in trials—but not to let vital forces be worn down, without which I could no longer gather up all my energy in order to continue.

August 17, 1969

In the church, we are reading the beginning of the Second Letter of Peter. My attitude in listening is rather that of someone who has just received a letter from one of Christ's contemporaries. Every word tells. Peter's faith—it counts, in life!

---

25. Brother Olivier (Jacques Perret, 1933–1986), French brother who spent many years with the brothers in Brazil.

August 18, 1969

Talk with a brother about what characterizes our vocation. In recent years we have given a great deal of importance to making everyone welcome. But what if this were to the detriment of some absolute bound up with our calling? Is it clear enough that the call constantly to follow Christ marks in us a line of separation?

August 19, 1969

This morning I glimpse Pablo Cano on the road.[26] "Hello, Señor Pablo! Vicente has left, you are on your own now." "Yes—all alone." We say good morning, then I hear him calling me back: "Brother Roger! Not alone; every day, our God is here." And he puts his hand over his heart.

A long walk with a brother. At the end of our conversation, he asks me, "What is most vital for you in our vocation?" At the moment, I see three values: prayer, love for the church, the search for justice.

August 20, 1969

Twenty-nine years ago today I discovered the village of Taizé. Within the community, I have always preferred this day to pass without being observed in any way.

From the very beginnings of Taizé, in this out-of-the-way spot, humanity, with or without God, victim of the powerful, has been present to me day after day.

---

26. In the 1950s, the community offered hospitality to an immigrant worker from the South of Spain, Pedro Cano, who was threatened with expulsion from France when he was dismissed from his work because of his union activities. His family soon came to join him, including his brother Pablo, who worked with the brothers.

1969

August 22, 1969

Yesterday and today, breakfast shared with young people. Their trust is touching. Are they aware of the struggle that is being fought within themselves by some of the brothers whom they admire?

Over the past few years, our relationship with these young people who come to our hill for a few days has changed. At first, we did not dare to go far in our exchanges with them. But today we touch on what lies at the center of our life. As these quiet, simple dialogues take place, every expression, every glance has its importance.

At the end of midday prayer I was speaking to a brother in the sacristy. A man came up to me and told me his name as though I knew him. He asked me to sign two of my books, something I always find hard, but I did not dare to refuse this sign of friendship. Quietly, in my ear, he whispered, "I had given up the priesthood, but I am going to be a priest again. The church is suffering." I don't know whether it was he or I who added, "The church is suffering! That is why we cannot abandon her." And he withdrew after promising to write.

August 23, 1969

I learn that Aldrin, the Apollo XI astronaut, took with him bread and wine consecrated at the Eucharist. Once on the moon, he prayed and took communion.

August 24, 1969

This morning, visit from a bishop from Italy with whom we were unacquainted, together with fifteen priests. Returning from the church, we talk of Christ's words, "This is my body."[27] I ask him, "Will the Catholic Eucharist remain closed to non-Catholics forever? Is no solution possible?" The bishop speaks to me in Latin of

---

27. Matt 26:26.

patience. The expression hurts, and I am surprised to find myself insisting: suppose this moment of history were not going to recur for a long while? I can already sense that all hopeful expectation is vanishing among the young.

August 26, 1969

Could it be that Christians are no longer bearers of good news? These days, each time I reach the religious news in the newspapers, I find nothing but sadness about the church. Over the last two years or so, I have seen the consequences of this. Men and women who once loved the church with every fiber of their being have begun to be suspicious of it. Then other men and women think it necessary to react by launching crusades. The sadness of the present time neutralizes any dynamism by which to move forward. What joyful news could motivate as many people as possible?

August 28, 1969

This evening our church is packed. Why do so many young people keep coming here? The best thing they can give us is to uphold our aspirations. But how can we uphold theirs? What else can we do but listen, trying to understand what animates them?

September 4, 1969

This morning, during the common prayer, all at once I was struck by the quality of my brothers and I was moved to the depths of my heart. They give their life, their whole life. They pay dearly the price of their commitment. I understand this better than anyone. Then I no longer know whether my admiration is for my brothers or for Christ, who has so set his mark on them.

1969

September 6, 1969

A young man asked to see me, to say he could not understand why we have given up the small communities of young people. His face, normally full of joy, was drenched with tears. It has stayed with me all day long.

I explained to him how, in a number of these communities where young people lived for a year or two under the same roof, the weakest elements had dominated. Out of generosity towards them the others—at the outset determined to live out the demands of the gospel—ultimately relativized the call of Christ. Gradually, the salt had lost its saltiness.[28]

This evening, I continue to question myself. I know that I am responsible to a great extent for the impasse we have reached with these young people. My idea had been: would it not be possible for young men and women to share our experience? Could they not live for a limited period the life we live for our whole lifetime?

Today, little church cells often spring up—fraternal, temporary. They melt into the ordinary life of society, in this way disappearing and becoming invisible. They belong to the underground movement of the church. They are found more or less everywhere. Like the cells of a body, they are born, subdivide, disappear. Some cease to exist for a time and then come into being again later.

Despite this possibility of their rising up in a new form,[29] I suffer from having had to put a stop to these small communities: was I really compassionate? Whenever I am obliged to say no in order to keep someone within the dynamic of the provisional, I am always afraid afterwards that I may have been less than merciful. Fortunately, today I was able to invite this particular young man

---

28. Matt 5:13.

29. In fact, these small provisional communities periodically resurfaced in the following years. During the preparation of the Council of Youth, young people were invited to form "cell groups" to help with the preparation, and in recent years, the community has organized dozens of "small provisional communities," whereby three young people from different countries are welcomed for a month or so by a parish or church in another city for an experience of prayer, service, and visits.

to eat with us and we laughed together: laughter makes us fully human.

September 8, 1969

A girl writes to me that, as a Christian, a revolution could lead her, if needed, to point a machine gun at her parents and kill them. So destruction has come to be lodged within her. Whether or not she actually commits this act "with a view to greater justice among human beings," as she puts it, the break in her is already complete.

September 9, 1969

A question written by one of the young people here: "You talk of suffering in the heart of the church. One can sense that these words capture precisely your own experience. For me it is something vague, outside of my experience, but your sharing in this suffering makes me ask myself questions. What really is this hurt at the church's heart? And then: what part can young laypeople play in a parable of Christ's love in the church and for the world?"

September 11, 1969

My mother begins her ninetieth year. Leaving the church today, she was surrounded by friends and she said to someone, who noted it down at once, "I know that in the next world I will be praising God constantly. And since praise is already the best part of my life here on this earth, what wonders of beauty I shall know then!"

September 12, 1969

Only reconciliation will bring a breath of fresh air and festivity to the church.

At the beginning of this century, Pope Pius X opened the Catholic Eucharist to little children and by so doing he unleashed a new burst of life that no one had dared hope for. He freed Christians from a conscience overburdened with scruples about receiving communion. Today, what Bishop of Rome—leading activator of reconciliation—will have the inner strength to make a simple gesture: to open the Catholic Eucharist to all the non-Catholics who seek in the Eucharist the reality of Christ's presence, and so to promote a new impetus of reconciliation?

September 29, 1969

Some people think that living in the country means being cut off from the world. But we bring the world with us, even in our deserts. Personally, nothing is easier for me than to live in the center of a large city, where I can be alone. The world is neither more nor less present there than in the peace of the fields.

October 17, 1969

A young Jesuit from Colombia asks me why the brothers are in general untouched by the theology of Bultmann,[30] "yet you are not men who refuse to consider any contemporary line of thought"?

What is at stake lies elsewhere and is so much more vital: to make the church and the earth places fit to live in. It lies in helping each person to grow in awareness of themselves, their thoughts, their worth, of the gifts of God within them, since God is present in every human being.

Our energies are limited, so a choice is necessary. What we lose on one side we gain on the other—where we believe the fate of humanity is being played out. Is anyone capable of fighting on several fronts at the same time?

---

30. Rudolf Bultmann (1884–1976), a German Bible scholar and theologian, distinguished radically, in the New Testament, the message for twentieth-century believers and the mythical expressions in which it was clothed. In 1941, concerning this program of "demythologization," he wrote, "One cannot use electric light and radios, call for medical care and modern clinics and, at the same time, believe in the world of spirits and miracles of the New Testament."

October 26, 1969

I am in the church, talking with a group of forty men, when suddenly I see one of them—quite young—collapse. Two of his friends carry him away and lay him at the foot of the altar, where he comes to himself. His drawn face, drenched in perspiration, shows that he is really not well. A doctor arrives and orders tea to be brought. But the sick man refuses, whispering "No, not here." He could not bear to take that drink at the spot where the Eucharist is celebrated. There is something noble in that attitude. "No, not here." I find everything in those three words; they fill me. And yet I am not at all shocked when young people, when there are crowds here in cold weather, bring their air mattresses and spend the night in the church, even at this very spot at the foot of the altar.

October 27, 1969

Some students ask me how they can work out a common rule for the year they are going to be living together. A rule! The term is so juridical! Yet I too used the word, twenty years ago, when I composed the short text that indicates the lines of force for our life. I suggest that they ask themselves questions starting from the context in which they find themselves. Like many young people, you refuse privileges. Yet your studies mean that you are certain to acquire them, and will perhaps lead you to positions of power. Are you going to prepare yourselves to dominate others, or to serve them?

October 28, 1969

This morning I asked myself what one word best characterized my life. I only came up with one answer: faithfulness.

In the village church, a number of young people, on their knees or lying flat on the floor, are searching for a moment's silence. And in burst some noisy women, anxious to visit everything. Someone points out that they are in a place of prayer. So out come rosaries, manipulated with gusto. And soon the chattering starts up again. In a word, they are protesting against the silence.

A very old woman is also there sometimes. She too prays the rosary—but how devoutly!

October 30, 1969

Outside the window, summer is still here. Today the light bathes everything in a clear blue.

Reynold[31] wants to talk about his work. How can he teach computer programming ten kilometers away and still maintain the priority of the community's prayer? I reassure him: in him there is no dichotomy between scientific research and our common creation. Whatever he may think, in fact he has managed to integrate the two. But he pays the price demanded by his searching.

November 7, 1969

Why this love for our house? The fire burning in the fireplace will keep my room warm all through the winter; since this morning drops of rain have been running down my windowpanes after months of drought. I have moved my desk close to the window. I cannot complete a single sentence without raising my eyes, so afraid I am of missing some change, the fringe of brightness around the long clouds, the patches of clear sky. The Far East in the sky above Burgundy!

November 8, 1969

Prayer? A world in itself. There are days when I feel like dancing to express my praise. I spoke about that with Madame Roosevelt.[32]

---

31. Brother Reynold (Jean-François Gallusser, 1945–) Swiss, French.

32. Jeannette Schlottman (1921–1974) was the third wife of Curtis Roosevelt (1930–2016), the grandson of Franklin Delano and Eleanor Roosevelt. The couple lived in France and were friends of the community.

The first time I met her, with her motionless features, I took her to be a Puritan of distinction. I was unaware that she was head of a school of dance in an American university. Then one day I saw her dance the *Stabat Mater* by Pergolesi: she was a different person.

I asked her about the use of dance in the church. She thought about it and gave me her reply some time later:

"We Westerners cannot simply ignore our inhibitions. Dancing during worship remains somehow artificial. But, adapted to our possibilities, quite imperceptible movements are enough to express it. In that way I can make even paralyzed people dance, by suggesting that they think of the movements and try to make them imperceptibly. Dance exists potentially within every person. The main thing is to live it with the imagination when there is no other way possible."

November 10, 1969

In me is a man who does not consider himself necessary. How is it that the confirmations that come from those I love simply spread over the surface, evaporating at the first blow?

The wind is blowing from the east, squall upon squall since early morning. The constant noise is tiring. I begin to long for the town.

November 12, 1969

To Macon to buy Christmas gifts. Coming down the last hill overlooking Macon, we have a view of the Jura Mountains as I have never seen them before, in all their depth.

Macon delights me as much today as on the day I first discovered it, one hot morning in August 1940. I have been through many towns. But the landscape along the Saone River, the road winding from the old bridge up to the Place de la Barre, the Place aux Herbes, friendly as none other at Christmas time—all these charm me and always express the same sense of welcome.

On the banks of the Saone, nasturtiums are still in flower. So there cannot have been any frost here, whereas at Taizé the gardens have gone dead over the last ten days beneath the freezing nights.

The return to Taizé means driving through the Bois Clair, then descending the blue valley and crossing empty countryside. The houses that are inhabited smile at me.

As I was waking this morning, the last dream of the night had me on a hill near Macon, at the top of a tower where, with my sister Genevieve and others, we were waiting for the sun to rise. First, from behind the Jura there appeared great fountains of light rising into the sky, then disappearing to be replaced by others, in a magnificent display of fireworks. Then the sun began to appear. And once more all was plunged into darkness. No one expressed surprise; such were the rules of the game. Vivid sense of joy at the vision.

I remind myself that I was born in the Jura, with just such a panorama before my eyes.

November 15, 1969

Picked chrysanthemums and marigolds in the garden. The late autumn: richly tinted skies, shades of violet and orange. And already, in the shelter of the house, the jasmine is promising its first flowers.

November 22, 1969

This afternoon we arrived in Rome.[33] We had been so looking forward to coming down through Italy and viewing the autumn. We found nothing but fog and pouring rain. Everything was

---

33. During the Second Vatican Council, to which Brothers Roger and Max were invited as guests of the Secretariat for Christian Unity, the community was able to rent an apartment on the Via del Plebiscito and welcomed many bishops and experts there for a meal during the sessions. After the Council, Brother Roger used to go to Rome with a few brothers each year, for dialogues with members of the Roman curia and a private audience with the pope.

suffused in a dusky light, whereas we had been expecting a glorious morning.

To the Corso for our first walk. At the opposite corner of the block in which we live is the Church of Santa Maria in Via Lata. It was built over the house where Saint Paul is said to have lived while under arrest. It is now open again, after being closed for restoration for years past. Angelo Roncalli, the future Pope John XXIII, lived in the apartment attached to this church as a young priest. He used to pray at this spot. Festival springs up in my heart.

In the church are several young men; a father with his small son hesitates at the threshold. We exchange a smile.

November 25, 1969

Today Pope John would have been eighty-eight years old. I am reading the letters he wrote to his family. Poverty-stricken priest that he was, he loved his people, supporting them as best he could.

The apartment is full of peace. This evening we were saying that even if it is different, silence is present here as at Taizé. In the courtyard, the water is spurting and bubbling in the fountain.

The moon pierces through the brownish-grey clouds. In the heart of a city it shows itself as nowhere else, above the mists tinted with all the accumulated smoke. Poetry does not die in the big cities.

Human beings are creative. If some of their discoveries pollute water and air, they will find ways of putting things right. Knowing as I do that the constant increase in population calls for prodigious means of development, I am confident in the creative capacity of human beings. Where technology is concerned, optimism prevails.

November 26, 1969

The bishop invited to this evening's meal is overflowing with benevolence. At table we laugh a great deal, so much so that I am obliged to add certain humorous details, to help one of my brothers with an uncontrollable fit of laughter. But everything is taken in good part. And in the exuberance of our conversation we touch on serious topics, topics I shall be taking up again during the many talks I shall have with all kinds of different partners in the days to come.

November 27, 1969

More and more convinced of one thing: our community will only be able to hold true if it can anticipate a communion with the Bishop of Rome, without repudiating our spiritual families of origin for all that.

November 28, 1969

Faithful to our Roman habits, we went at about eleven PM to take the last letters to the central post office. With me came a young brother due to set off the next morning for the North East of Brazil. He will have to rise at dawn and, because he did not want to wake me then, I had already given him my blessing and we had said goodbye when we decided to go out for our walk.

Only two minutes before we reached the house again, he told me something he had been keeping to himself for months past: a mutual friend, a priest, had asked to be relieved of his ministry.

In a few seconds I saw a whole long story before my eyes: discovery at the Council of a young priest from Latin America, open-faced, with a wide smile, deep eyes with an inkling of sadness. His bishop could not have been more generous and the son was full of regards for the father. Loving both of them, I tried to understand.

What is that priest going to become once out of the priesthood? This event is so hard to bear that I find I have suddenly grown older. Once alone in my room, tears flow as I try to grasp the mystery of that life.

November 30, 1969

Sunday in Rome—a long walk on the Palatine, letters that are a joy to write, the telephone call from Taizé, an excursion through the crowded streets, in places swarming with people, the meal begun with a meditation on the gospel by a young Latin American, a prayer at eleven PM in Santa Maria in Via Lata—all things that go to make up a day filled with festival.

December 3, 1969

Certain present-day trends incline towards a pluralism without unanimity. In the church the result is a body without a heart. And immediately a struggle ensues between those who are interested solely in the diversity of the different members and those who, as a reaction to this, want to impose a heart out of all proportion. In a monastic community this would mean that sooner or later there would be no way of living a parable of unity.

December 5, 1969

A festive morning, with an appointment at the Secretariat of State. In the Vatican there is a strong family spirit, inevitable given the warm humanity of the Italians. The two elevator operators are both friends for me. At the end of the gallery a uniformed Swiss guard salutes. "Did we meet during the Council?" I ask. "No," he replies, "but I was with you at Geneva on the boat carrying the pope." An old bishop is sitting there, tired and looking sad. We share a few words. Then I am addressed by two priests who know me; one is the young bishop of S. in central Italy. After my meeting, I take the elevator in the company of an Italian priest who tells me he has been to Taizé several times. On the way out, still more signs of friendship from those who welcome visitors, all very simple but very human—the face of God in these faces that are poor.

December 7, 1969

At times, in the silence of my Roman room, I realize how certain reforms in the church may only affect the surface of things. It is not those who say "Lord, Lord" who do the Father's will.[34] And it is not those who say "reform, *aggiornamento*[35]" who are the most receptive. It is good to wash the outside of the cup, but what will become of us if it is not clean within?[36]

December 9, 1969

Letter to a Latin American priest:

"I am with you step by step in the formidable struggle you have undertaken for those whom others—including we Christians—have left behind. In going to live with the poor, your service goes beyond what is humanly possible...

"I recall your inner combat. And my thought is: true, reforms are essential for the People of God, but only on one condition, that people themselves be transformed.

"I meet men advanced in years who find it hard to see the need for the renewals. But they are full of goodness and with them the gifts of the heart, pastoral concern, make up for many failings. Such men do not hinder those who entrust themselves to them.

"But at present, others in the church are applauding the reforms. Younger, even much younger, they think that by consenting with their minds they are fully within the *aggiornamento*. And yet, some of these middle-aged men, lacking any human or pastoral sensibility, will not let themselves be interrogated by present failures. Far from encouraging, their attitude holds back and imprisons the most generous Christians.

---

34. See Matt 7:21.

35. *Aggiornamento*, literally "updating," was a word used by Pope John XXIII to indicate one of the objectives of the Second Vatican Council. The Italian word entered the Christian vocabulary of the day without needing to be translated.

36. See Luke 11:39.

"I am at that stage of my life and you are about to enter it. How can we defend ourselves against this lack of understanding, against harshness towards anybody, and particularly towards those who cause harm to others?"

December 17, 1969

Today, private audience with Paul VI. Full of joy, the Pope's welcoming words were so generous towards Taizé that I dare not repeat them. Then our conversation begins, and it goes far. The Pope offers to celebrate Mass for Taizé on December 31.

December 29, 1969

Returned to Taizé ten days ago with bronchial pneumonia. The combined effect of the illness and my work was to rob me of all my strength. The two brothers who are doctors stressed that I was to remain in bed, even for the Christmas midnight Mass. But that evening one of them was himself confined to bed with the flu, and the other was on duty at the hospital at Macon. So I was free to go against instructions. And here I am on my feet, ready to carry on.

Each day I remain in the church, talking with young people. One question was, "What does sin mean?" It is not an easy thing to talk about today. The psychological sciences have taught us how in every person there lies a predetermined pattern of disorder. Children have suffered at the hands of their parents, who themselves were traumatized in their early upbringing. The individual finds himself relieved of a burden of responsibilities resulting from the whole lineage of his ancestors. So what then is sin? It is there whenever I deliberately prefer my own will to that of Christ, whenever instead of serving others I make them my slaves.

December 31, 1969

The final hours of the year, and I am filled with a flood of joy. I live in such thankfulness that the trials of the moment are light to bear.

The sight of countless young faces—those from different countries here at Taizé—persuades me that with them we shall be able to build something for humankind and for the church.

To share in the trials of the church and to love her still more because of them.

Gratitude for Hector and Ghislain, our first two Catholic brothers.[37] Gratitude for each of my brothers without exception.

I believe that I discover the foundation of my joy in consenting to the fact that one day I shall leave life on earth for a life that will have no end. I am not interested in knowing what God's eternity will look like; I have better things to do than to conjure up images of paradise. But the knowledge that I will be able to close my eyes in peace and encounter Christ is a source of festival. Consenting to one's own death opens towards a flood of life.

---

37. The first Roman Catholic brothers were able to enter the community in 1967, with the tacit approval of the archbishop of Paris, François Cardinal Marty. Hector Torres was from Colombia and had come to France to study sociology there; he soon returned to his country of origin. Brother Ghislain (Jean-Paul Mazure, 1942–) was a medical doctor from Belgium.

1970

1970 was above all the year which saw, at Easter, the announcement of a planned "Council of Youth," which would be prepared in the following four years before opening in August of 1974. The journal entries for this year recount numerous conversations with young people striving for greater justice in society, particularly from Latin America, as well as with priests attempting to come to terms with the turmoil in the postconciliar church. Brother Roger's pen, however, periodically describes the scenery and the weather at Taizé, as if he found in this evocation of the natural world a respite from the painful tensions in society and in the church. Two journeys to other countries also marked this year—to the South of Spain in February, and to Rome in December, including a memorable visit to the South of Italy—two opportunities for the prior of Taizé to discover the face of Christ in the poor and forgotten.

January 1, 1970

The year of 1970 will be the one in which we shall dare new things.

Today's dialogue with the young people was a real boxing match. The ones peppering me with questions pushed me to my limits. I was laughing inwardly, but sometimes it took my breath away.

We spoke of the role of Mary today. She, a woman, is going to lead us to make a discovery. The church has left it to men to take all the initiatives. Mary teaches us that initiatives are the concern of women as well. She is the foremost witness of the church, and invites man to rid himself of his self-sufficiency, his authoritarianism, in order to collaborate with God.

The last question dealt with our contacts with the working classes. My reply: in our fraternities far away, there are new possibilities. But in our region, the gates of the nearby factories were closed to us when, living in a *fraternité* thirty kilometers from Taizé,[1] we were considered to be too lucid about the conditions of many workers there. Since then it has been impossible to find a job in any local factory. Yet every day there are brothers who go off to work nearby.[2]

What I should have added is that, as the new year begins, I cannot see who is offering any real solution for greater justice. I have no more confidence in liberal democracies led by oligarchies than in systems dominated by police repression, as in certain socialist countries. How to foster a leap forward towards a just society?

---

1. In the mining town of Montceau-les-Mines, from 1951 to 1953.

2. At that time, Brother Robert was working as a doctor in Cormatin, Brother Alain in an agricultural cooperative, and Brother Reynold taught computer science at Cluny.

January 2, 1970

Marc[3] is back. He relates his mother's last day. Without saying anything to her family, she announces to someone there that she will die during the day. The day goes by as usual. Those present pray compline with her, as they do every evening. She prays more fervently for many of those entrusted to her. Then she says good night to her husband and collapses: death had come.

Two days later her husband, an unpretentious man, sees her alongside him. She is resplendent with light and insists, "Do not be sad. Go peacefully through these days. Know that I am no longer of earth but of heaven."

January 5, 1970

In the presence of others, a young Italian couple asks me to say a few words meant just for them. He is a worker. His wife is on the staff of a labor union. The question intimidates me a little and I would prefer to avoid it. Their expressions are so open and appealing that I venture to ask them: you are attached to Christ, but how can you serve him together also within his body, the church? That means not living suspended between earth and heaven, but with both feet planted firmly on the ground.

January 6, 1970

Talked with Italians and Spaniards, all involved in the working world. The same concern about the church as yesterday. Of course, loving the church for its own sake would lead to disaster. For "reasons of state," what injustices have not been committed in the course of history? Similarly, for "reasons of church," what has not been done? Loving the church in isolation, without Christ, would lead to intransigence. But loving Christ alone, without his

---

3. Brother Marc (Heinz Rudolf, 1931–), Swiss German brother who worked as an artist in different media. He spent many years with the brothers in Japan and Korea.

body, encourages a narrowness within us. Loving Christ, loving the church: the two are one. These words challenge me ceaselessly.

January 7, 1970

Have set on the mantelpiece in my room a calendar brought back from Italy. Each day's date is very big, printed in red. In this way I can remember the day to be lived, today, January 7, and no other— a day given for friendship, peace, and joy. True, a bad letter has arrived, but it has not been able to put out the latent fire.

January 8, 1970

Yesterday evening, conversation with a young poet. Listening to him, everything around us took on new life and, in this cold winter, I could sense in the row of trees young shoots stirring beneath the dead leaves.

January 10, 1970

The race to succeed, the ambition that lies behind it: what devastation that is for Christians! When someone has no other means of regaining confidence in himself, he is heading for dislocation; he drains away the best of himself.

January 11, 1970

Listen, always listen. Jo, an African economist, speaks of this in a new way. Listening, he says, is in Africa the role of the chief. Surrounded by others who help him to understand properly, he listens to each in turn. And then a direction becomes clear. Appearances notwithstanding, the head of a tribe often has a highly demanding life to live, since he is obliged to listen to all.

January 12, 1970

These last weeks, Alain[4] has been coming home every day with new burdens that are almost unbearable. For sixteen years now, so much energy spent sharing in the transformation of the living conditions of the least well-to-do farmers. In the evening, I listen to him for a moment. What else can I do but share his present worries?

January 14, 1970

My sister Yvonne, just back from the Congo, had this story to tell about her four-year-old granddaughter Stephanie. She discovered that, in the house next door, an African boy of the same age had to spend the whole day with the servants, without his parents. He cried constantly. So every evening, at nightfall, Stephanie would go to the bottom of the garden where a small hole in the wall opened on to the grounds next door. The little boy would be waiting for her and they held hands through the opening, having no common language to speak.

January 15, 1970

For the past two days a bishop from Brazil has been here. Once again I am given an insight into the treasury of faith, of sensitivity, into the creative capacity of the Christians from that continent.

The relationship between us has been falsified by centuries of ecclesiastical exportation to Latin America. But today in Latin America, women and men are arising who will come to evangelize in us all that remains steeped in self-sufficiency, paganism, and unbelief.

---

4. See p. 11, note 8.

January 16, 1970

Letter to a young Italian Catholic:

"To live Christ for others. To take part concretely, by giving all one's life, in the reawakening of a vocation proper to the Catholic church—to be a leaven of fraternal and visible unity within the whole human community. Surely that is our call and, henceforth, our common path."

January 19, 1970

At this beginning of the week of prayer for Christian unity, denominational inertia is more apparent than ever.

Yesterday, many people from the region were gathered in our church. The priests were sitting among my brothers. The diocesan bishop preached. We live equally close every year. Yet we still remain apart for the Eucharist, and we all believe in it with a common faith.

But optimism still does not desert me. The impossible opens the way to the possible.

January 20, 1970

This day, January 20, calls my father to mind. Twenty-four years ago he was struck down with an illness that was to take his life within a few days.

A grey day; the weather could hardly be gloomier. But however overcast the sky is, there is always a brighter patch somewhere.

I strive to live as a man familiar with his inevitable portion of solitude.

January 23, 1970

Marked by conversations with someone so tense that all I could do was listen attentively and very receptively. At such moments I sometimes wonder: are these situations part of God's plan? This morning the reply would have been: the church carries along with it all our humanity and a person's inner tensions are part of it.

January 27, 1970

A short stay in Paris. Evening spent with a young astrophysicist from Bombay.[5] I share with him this question which never leaves me: now that I sense Easter drawing near, I wonder if we shall have the strength to go ahead in a commitment with the young. I would like to give up the idea of a council of youth.

After he left, I continued the same reflection alone: as far as I am concerned, nothing is disastrous, not even my own death. But I am not the only one involved in all this. Should I put a stop to what we have begun? Would giving up be an act of cowardice towards the young? Have I looked closely enough to see if everything necessary is ready?[6]

January 28, 1970

Reading certain writings, even in very serious periodicals, how many invitations there are to lose touch! The ideas are there. Then, with a little imagination, a web of gilded alibis is woven—more than enough to take leave of reality.

January 29, 1970

If I am with a nonbeliever, is the presence of Christ excluded? His presence is other, more I cannot grasp.

---

5. Moiz Rasiwala (1937–), born in Bombay to a Muslim family, studied astrophysics in Germany and France, and became a Christian without ever rejecting his roots. He was active in the preparation of the Council of Youth and spent time in Taizé, helping with the international meetings there. Later he settled in the West of France with his wife and children and was ordained a Catholic deacon while maintaining close ties with the Taizé Community.

6. See Luke 14:28.

January 30, 1970

A young man asks me, "How do you see the service of authority in today's church? How do you conceive it for yourself, as prior of Taizé?"

Authority has too often been identified with a temporal power, but in the church it is first of all communion. Authority is neither monarchical nor democratic; it is pastoral.

Personally I see my ministry as a service of unity. To be prior of Taizé is, in my eyes, to be a man of communion.

Christ says of the shepherd that he gives his life, that he exposes it before the ravenous wolf ever ready to divide.[7] I need a shred of the courage of Christ not to give up in the face of difficulty, not to flee but, on the contrary, to foster unity, sometimes to arbitrate in situations, and also to keep those who are mine in communion with the whole church.

Power is of no interest to me in exercising this ministry. I simply know that our community's vocation is to live, each day, a parable of unity and that it cannot do so without a servant, the prior, who sums up the whole.

Such a service of unity does not set the one exercising it at the top of a pyramid, but right in the midst of all.

February 1, 1970

Throughout the day, wherever I go and whomever I may be with, I find ways of watching what is happening in the sky. So much creativity constantly in action, so many shades of gold set off by brilliant greys—joyfulness wells up inside me, and it is not so hard to bear the burden of contradictions.

---

7. See John 10:1–18.

1970

February 2, 1970

These days, the manifold pressures on me are so contradictory that I find myself wondering: am I blind? Is my own view of things an illusion? A deep underlying stillness makes it possible for me to withstand the assaults day after day.

February 3, 1970

The southern window admits a first trace of spring: far off, a fringe of changing light borders the hills of Cluny.[8] I would not want to miss a moment of this promise of delight.

February 4, 1970

Human beings are bearers of Christ, but that does not mean that Christ can be reduced to an anthropocentric dimension. That would turn him into a mere projection of ourselves.

February 5, 1970

A brother hands me a paper on which he has noted the conclusion of an inner debate. The most demanding part of what he lives for Christ brings him still closer to his brothers. Perhaps it is the awareness of his poverty that gives him such transparence.

February 6, 1970

Talk with a young Italian. He has often been here without our having met. At Christmas, when I was talking with hundreds of young people, I noticed him. Why? I could not say. From our first words,

---

8. A town twelve kilometers from Taizé, site of the Benedictine abbey founded in 910, one of the great centers of Christian spirituality in the Middle Ages. After many centuries of decline, the abbey was finally destroyed during the French revolution.

his transparence made me sure that he would be the first young European to participate in the intercontinental team, to announce at Easter the news that is taking shape.

February 9, 1970

A man in his thirties, his eyes like burning coals, interrupted me yesterday during the dialogue in the church, to ask me how to react to unfaithfulness towards Christ. Was my reply disappointing? I said: Lent is approaching. It is a time set apart for examining the inner self. Forty days of celebration to rediscover the joy of forgiveness.

This morning I saw the same man. He is a priest, and I understand what is at stake in his struggle. I could find nothing more telling than this to affirm: his yes, pronounced one day before Christ and the church, involved, as it does for everyone, certain psychological motivations. But a vocation cannot simply be reduced to its psychological components. His yes cannot be a total mistake; it remains the yes of faith.

At the same dialogue a teenager, sitting near the back, asked me timidly, "Brother, who is Christ for you?" I had never been asked that in public before. I ask him his name. He is called Alain, and comes from the local mining region. I suggest that he repeat the question in the microphone. He expresses himself anew, in a strong local accent.

For me, Christ is the one by whom I live, but also the one for whom I, with you, am searching.

February 16, 1970

For several days now, I have known that at Easter we shall have television cameras to transmit on Eurovision, live, the moment when the Council of Youth is announced. The time is fixed necessarily in the late morning. I have only to think of it to lose all joy. The young people will be coming primarily to celebrate the resurrection. That is the main thing. We cannot risk troubling the Easter morning liturgy by pressures due to the technical demands of a live broadcast two hours later. Today we agreed to telephone the producer, to ask him to put the broadcast off until Easter afternoon. He cannot. In that case, we shall give up the Eurovision; it will be for another day. Once the decision was made, it was as though the field lay wide open: free to be spontaneous!

February 17, 1970

There are Christians who want their concept of society to prevail by violence. Others strive hard to impose a stifling doctrinal rigidity. And others, at present, are banding together against pornography. Would Christ call us to organize ourselves in order to impose our views?

Those crusading against eroticism, for example: what motives are they obeying? Do they want to protect others by a simple outward morality that is incapable of modifying what lies within? But purity of heart is not satisfied with the appearance of wholesomeness. It delves deeper, to rid us of hypocritical or calculating attitudes. And what if some were motivated by frustration? Working out a morality on the basis of unsatisfied desires has nothing to do with the gospel.

February 23, 1970

Eight days spent traveling through Spain. Days overflowing with happiness. The liveliness of the Spanish people, especially in the South, is invigorating.

At Malaga, in the evening we join the crowds filling the streets in the city center. We make our way with difficulty through the mass of humanity. The wide paving stones, smooth as a skating rink, incite us to slide rather than walk. Out of all the confused uproar pierce the shrill notes of an Andalusian song.

We go into a church. Young people are playing rhythms on the guitar to accompany unknown tunes. An old layman reads the Old Testament, a girl wearing a long dark red coat goes to read the epistle. Where am I? In the far south of Spain where, even in the church, nothing is as it used to be. I have never been at a Mass using rhythmic music and now here I am, at the edge of Europe, gripped by its expressive force.

February 24, 1970

We have reached one of the goals of our journey. Leaving the main road at Bassa, we set out down a narrow but still passable road and finally go thirty kilometers along a gravelly track. The further we go, the stronger become the wild golden tints of the earth. Three times we descend to the bottom of vast hollows scooped out of the plateau by centuries of erosion.

Campo Camara, a high-perched village near the Sierra Sagra. Walking through the streets we hasten to the home of Pedro Cano.[9] The entrance—door and window combined—stands half-open. I push it further and see him, huddled on a low chair against the hearth. He is there in the shadows, even more gaunt than a few years ago. He stretches out his arms to us: his eyes afire, he grasps our hands in his own. Not just the family but all the neighbors as well are squeezed into the one narrow room with its earthen floor. He insists on our taking something to eat. Only the head of the family and we, his three guests, are entitled to the bacon, wine, and beer.

The shadows of the night come on. It is time to leave. Once back on the asphalt road, I notice that all three of us are silent. What could we have to say to one another? We have seen a face of Christ.

Max[10] has fallen asleep, though normally he can always find tales to fill the car with our laughter. Patrick accelerates, nothing

9. See p. 28, note 26.
10. Brother Max (Thurian, 1921–1996), one of the first four brothers of the community, theologian, with Brother Roger observer at the Second Vatican

but the hum of the engine. To speed through the night brings back a dream of my childhood.

March 12, 1970

Four days at Constantinople. Afterwards, what raises my hopes is the awareness that an eighty-six-year-old man, Patriarch Athenagoras, with so few means at his disposal and in a complex political situation, can have an enormous impact both close at hand and far away.

I have heard words I cannot repeat. They burn and have great weight. He, servant of the unity of the Orthodox world, has the greatness of the truly generous.

Until my last hour, I shall see him as he was when we left. He held his hands high as though presenting the eucharistic chalice and repeated once more: "The cup and the breaking of the bread, there is no other solution. Remember..."

March 14, 1970

My heart bleeds. Philippe's death, on February 25, has caught up with me at last.[11] At first I had simply seen the event in the context of the communion of saints, but after three weeks the humanity within me strikes back.

Philippe, a brother of the beginnings. With him everything always ended in laughter. Ever since the news reached me in Spain, I have been wondering: what is the meaning of this unexpected heart attack in a man so young? Why this tearing apart? Like so many others confronted with a separation, I accept my lack of any reply.

Council, active in ecumenical movements such as *La groupe de Dombes* and Faith and Order. Ordained a Roman Catholic priest in Naples in 1988 at his own initiative.

11. Brother Philippe (Brandon, 1922–1970), French, died of a sudden illness in Chicago after three years spent living with the Taizé brothers there.

March 23, 1970

There are young people here from every continent. Together we are going to announce something new. I repeat to myself: beyond the event, God is waiting for us. Once we have launched it, we shall hold firm. Among the young people present is Maximinio, a young peasant from the Northeast of Brazil. One of the poorest of the poor, when he arrived at Lisbon he had no jacket nor overcoat. He wonders how our stomachs can take three meals a day.

March 28, 1970

Holy Saturday. I asked Maximinio to sit at my place, on my stool in the middle of the brothers, for midday prayer. An unusual gesture, which was not understood by all.

March 29, 1970 – Easter Day

The "joyful news"[12] has been announced; the Council of Youth will be the instrument by which to put it into practice.

Last night, I woke up with this thought: you will never manage it, the words will refuse to come out.

This afternoon, as I took the microphone to announce the Council of Youth, a young Italian whispered in my ear, "Speak up, Brother Roger; you must proclaim the announcement of the Council of Youth." How well he knows me!

---

12. This short text, written by Brother Roger with an intercontinental team of young adults, was the basis for the international meetings and visits that prepared the Council of Youth: "The risen Christ comes to quicken a festival in the innermost heart of man. He is preparing for us a springtime of the church, a church devoid of means of power, ready to share with all, a place of visible communion for all humanity. He is going to give us the imagination and courage to open up a way of reconciliation. He is going to prepare us to give our lives so that man may no longer be victim of man."

1970

April 1, 1970

Keep a heart at peace in the midst of an enthusiastic crowd these last three days. And peace of heart, too, when criticisms start surging up.

Monday evening, Maximinio left for home. He is a witness I lean on. I remain attentive to the blessing he gave as he set out: "Receive my blessing. Blessed be the heart that is poor, reconciled and unified by Jesus Christ." Before leaving me he also said, "*Meu coraçao está cheio de felicidade.*"[13]

During these days, we have seen with our own eyes the faces of "man victim of man"; we have heard appeals rising from the depths of the abyss: Maximinio, Ann, Michael, Maria, Edna.

After the announcement of the Council of Youth, I had expected all kinds of misunderstandings to arise. I was wrong.

In my youth, fear sometimes prevailed. I could not see the reason for so many fruitless struggles. From 1948 to 1960 that same fear returned once again, this time because of the battle for the unity of the church. Today, having reached my present age, may I keep the joy that ever remains!

April 8, 1970

"It is not those who see God who are saints, but those who believe in Him," wrote Saint Teresa of Avila.

April 14, 1970

At Geneva, during our visit to the World Council of Churches, there were moments of intensity—the prayer, the two meals. But the exchanges always remain less than what we would like to communicate to one another. One can sense there the impact of secularization.

---

13. "My heart is full of happiness."

April 16, 1970

These days, when I put out my light before falling asleep, a thought goes through my mind: perhaps this is the last time you will fall asleep on earth, the last time eyes will close which have been filled with the joy of earth's colors and harmonies.

April 18, 1970

We are witnessing a vast process of transformation of the human consciousness.

When asked to consider the people or things of the past, even the recent past, young people often employ a critical approach—a protest. This worldwide phenomenon is true of the youth of all societies, Christian or not. Like people everywhere, they suffer from a doubt about themselves and to find reassurance they affirm themselves brutally.

Aware of the enormous present-day increase in population, they are discovering the strength of their numbers. Because of this, some feel that they could have a share in the exercise of power, or even simply take charge by violence, in order to create the more just society to which they aspire.

Then, too, it is by protesting that youth judges the real worth of their elders. They want to find out if they can really give their trust.

If we let this new attitude shake or paralyze us, we may no longer have any way of tackling basic questions together, and then dialogue breaks down.

April 19, 1970

All day I have been full of what I was thinking about yesterday. Who would have said, five years ago, that today I should have so many conversations with protesting Christians? I remember the first shocks we experienced at Taizé, during a huge gathering of young people. It was in 1966, long before the events of May 1968.

1970

A brother has just reminded me that in the same year, 1966, I wrote at the beginning of *Unanimity in Pluralism*: "To desire pluralism for its own sake, without a unanimity in what is fundamental, is to accept—sooner or later—the death of faith on the earth. Scattered apart, people are given over to mutual strife." I cannot remember writing those words.

With the perspective that age is gradually giving me, I have come to distinguish two distinct expressions of protest among young Christians.

There is a small number for whom protest has become an end in itself. If dialogue is undertaken, there is a risk of unleashing irrational and uncontrollable impulses within them.

But then there is the vast majority: those who allow the gospel to protest within them. They live by the Word that challenges them. How can we be attentive to them? I often wonder whether the apostle Peter could also have been referring to them when he said, "Listen to the prophetic word!"[14]

These young Christians are fascinated by all that concerns prayer and faith, but they are afraid of being manipulated. They find it hard to understand why others distrust them and set up so many protective barriers. No matter how good the reasons lying behind the warnings they are given, these have just the opposite effect to that intended. How can an indispensable complementarity be achieved between charisms and institutions, spontaneity and continuity?

April 21, 1970

Beneath a leaden sky, spring is here. I no longer see it; I hear it.

While I am talking with the former bishop of Autun,[15] a brother brings me the newspaper. Good news: the pope, addressing

---

14. 2 Pet 1:19.

15. Lucien-Sidroine Lebrun (1896–1985), bishop from 1940 to 1966 of the diocese of Autun, where Taizé is located. He attended all four sessions of the Second Vatican Council and there discovered, to his surprise, the worldwide impact of Taizé.

the crowd on Sunday at midday from his window, spoke about the difficulties of ecumenism, then about the Orthodox churches. After noting that there were positive signs, Paul VI spoke these words: "We look towards Taizé with affectionate respect."

April 28, 1970

Admiration, astonishment: these Gospel values open onto "enthusiasm"—literally, "being seized by God."

April 29, 1970

Yesterday I received Father Voillaume.[16] I remind him how in 1949 we were awaiting the postulancy of the Little Brothers of Jesus at Taizé.[17] But the Catholic hierarchy refused to hear of it. At that time, I was conscious that their coming could lead to our living a common undertaking. I said to myself: why create a new community when the Little Brothers of Charles de Foucauld come so close? Unable to welcome them, we were obliged to mature without them the ecumenical vocation that has brought us to our present position. But I view them with the same admiration today as on the first day.

We speak of the preparation of the Council of Youth. Father Voillaume proposes a *fraternité* in common on another continent involving four or five brothers. To think we have had to wait twenty years for this!

Together we went to the village church, where the eucharistic reserve is kept. Can I write this? I have no wish for wonders that are beyond me but light—inner and outer—filled the place where we were. I did not linger but rose, so greatly do I fear putting God to the test.

---

16. René Voillaume (1905–2003), founder in 1933 of the Little Brothers of Jesus, in the spirit of Charles de Foucauld.
17. In other words, young men wishing to become Little Brothers of Jesus would come to Taizé to explore that vocation.

May 6, 1970

Yesterday evening, the birth of a child who is dear to me from the first: Jean-Christophe Rémy, a great-nephew, my sixty-seventh. Christophe, bearer of Christ: and I know he will be.

May 7, 1970

A man in his forties, unsmiling, asks me how to find a second breath so as to hold firm in his vocation. For me there is only one way: return time and time again to the first beginnings. At that moment, the decision to give all one's life scattered thick clouds and made happiness burst forth. Welcoming afresh the initial discoveries into one's life remains a festive source that allows, not just a second breath, but a whole series of new breaths, until death.

May 10, 1970

Yesterday I was thinking: the Easter season is almost over. It went by in a flash. And today I received this note from a young man: "Community prayer is a life; it is not undergone, but lived. It is a celebration, not a discipline. . . . The silence is intense, palpable, so authentic as to be almost sacramental. More than in personal devotion where I only encounter the God of Good Friday, I have rediscovered the Christ of Easter."

May 11, 1970

Faithful to my old habit of listening to the same piece of music for several days in a row, as I write I am playing a record of Bach's D-minor oboe concerto. In it I hear every human supplication, and a reply. I hear in colors. This music is tinged with orange, as has been the year that ends for me today.

At this moment, 5:30 PM, I can see, through my northern window, a clear sky filling with enormous white cumulus clouds. High up the wind is blowing, yet the lime trees close by are motionless. The wind drives the clouds one against another, then scatters them again. And I am here, my head raised, swallowed up in happiness.

May 12, 1970

On this birthday, I am overwhelmed by the attentiveness of my brothers, and also of my family. This morning, a letter from Robert.[18] That brother is ill again. During his long journey across Latin America, his eyes have seen the face of trampled humanity. But, in his solitude far away, he has also understood the dynamism of the younger generation. And at this very moment, I receive a birthday telegram sent by him from Buenos Aires: "May your festival have no end."

The following entries were published in 1973 in a volume entitled Lutte et contemplation *(Struggle and Contemplation).*

May 14, 1970

Setting out, not knowing where we are heading. . . . It is a month and a half now since the Council of Youth was announced. We have cut our moorings. Who knows, perhaps we and the young people will be able to head out on the open seas and join with a great number of people throughout the world.

May 15, 1970

A fascination with the sky, whether grey or radiant, is with me as soon as I wake. This is something characteristic of many people who were born in the country. Up rapidly to see what the weather

---

18. Brother Robert (Giscard, 1922–1993), the fifth brother to enter the community and the first Frenchman. A medical doctor, he was also an avid musician and, with the composer and organist Jacques Berthier, created the short musical phrases known throughout the world as the songs of Taizé.

is like. Light rain has dampened the ground. The trees on the terrace are gleaming under the cool showers. The lemon balm is in bud, about to burst open. The sky is overcast but the earth sings.

May 16, 1970

What kind of adventure have we embarked upon? The preparation of the Council of Youth is bound to be a long march through a wilderness. The festival of the paschal mystery presupposes an inner combat that could overwhelm us at times. "When it suffers, the heart finds a way out and begins to live anew."[19] That same festival activates a struggle together with those who are oppressed: it would soon burn itself out if we tried to live it for ourselves alone.

May 17, 1970

Could the call to reconciliation encourage passivity, a life without struggle? No, never! The gospel does not lead to tranquility. Being reconciled with oneself, as with others, presupposes that we consent to tensions and struggles. By neutralizing or fleeing situations of crisis, vital energy is destroyed. Passing through crises, looking beyond . . . : this a path that takes us far.

May 18, 1970

Pinned to my wall these words from the Cuban writer José Martí:[20] *"Cuando otros lloran sangre, ¿qué derecho tengo yo para llorar lagrimas?"* (When others are weeping blood, what right have I to weep tears?)

---

19. Quotation from Miguel de Unamuno (1864–1936), a Spanish writer and philosopher, author of *The Tragic Sentiment of Life*. Brother Roger was familiar with this work from seeing it on the bedside table of his grandmother.

20. José Martí (1853–1895), thinker, journalist, and poet, killed during the Cuban struggle for independence.

May 19, 1970

A great many young people, involved in struggles for justice, are experiencing discouragement. Buoyed up in recent years by an extravagant hope, many of them are now victims of bitterness or skepticism, both of them forms of self-destruction. In the presence of this kind of inner collapse, how can we communicate some optimism? There is a new element: we are capable, believers and nonbelievers together, of a common creation.

May 20, 1970

To follow Christ, in our consumer society, becomes something heroic.

May 21, 1970

The full moon bathes the valley in a peaceful light. On recent nights, when everyone is asleep, I have gone walking along the path leading to the hermitages. Just now, when I was back, I thought: in a century's time others will go for the same walks in the night. I can imagine nothing about them, but it will be the same ground and the same soft light. Will the same searching be in them?

May 24, 1970

Visit from Dom Helder Camara.[21] No sooner has he arrived than he declares, "Roger, I am afraid for the community when you die." Not at all expecting such words, I assure him that there is nothing to fear.

A little later, Dom Helder tells how happy he was to hear of the announcement of the Council of Youth, and adds, "When I

---

21. Helder Camara (1909–1999), archbishop of Olinda and Recife in the Northeast of Brazil, one of the leading figures of the Second Vatican Council, active in the struggle for justice and human rights alongside the poor and a personal friend of Brother Roger's.

learned who had announced it, I said to myself: 'Roger could do that.'"

I ask him what he thinks is most important for young Europeans. He points to the long table laid out under the trees to welcome the Portuguese immigrants invited here to meet him: "In the countries of Europe there are vast islands of poverty. The Third World is here too in your midst, among the poor you have in Europe, the immigrants who come seeking work, who are more or less well received and who often live in wretched living conditions. In Europe you are happy to talk about the development of the Third World, but do not forget your own development problems. If you do not work for a solution here, you justify the great gap between rich and poor in our countries."

Dom Helder! Eight years have passed since we first got to know one another. Never a shadow in our friendship—a rare friendship, with a man of many faces, a man like quicksilver, full of warmth in his vivid language and his gestures.

I see him in my mind's eye, when he came to share a meal with us in Rome. He would take a paper out of his pocket, put on his glasses, and read us part of the speech he was currently preparing. At such times he became another man, one who strives to convince, to communicate some fundamental ideas. Every address he gave during the Council was first read out, I think, at our table.

May 25, 1970

Life in community makes it possible to gain an education from one another. Simply by being interested in the work of one's brothers, there is no telling the treasures that are in easy reach. Being enriched by a process of osmosis!

May 26, 1970

Rediscovering our region: unknown landscapes just beyond our enclosure. Now that a gateway has been opened, as we have always wished, it is at last possible to leave the house and walk northwards along the hill in solitude, while there is so much activity close by.

May 27, 1970

The forecasts of doom arising from the pollution of air or water are intolerable. Affluent countries have affluent problems! Modern technology will find the necessary solutions. Let us not let our energies get diverted into worrying about that. It would lead us to focus on our own selves, and there are better things to be done.[22]

June 2, 1970

Why do exceptional people so often find it hard to get along with each other? This is sometimes explained as a form of rivalry and its consequence: the inability to be oneself. Those who are jealous do not believe that they are complementary to others; they prefer to copy them. Such forms of imitation are invariably caricatures.

June 3, 1970

To love, we do not have at our disposal a particularly wide range of impulses. We make use of the same flows of affection for human love or for the love of Christ.

---

22. Like all of us, Brother Roger was a man of his time, with a deep confidence in technological progress, which by today's standards could appear excessive. It was undoubtedly not easy, in 1970, to judge the relevance and the urgency of the ecological question, and especially to see its relationship to justice in the world. This was brilliantly demonstrated in Pope Francis's 2015 encyclical *Laudato Si'*, which Brother Roger would undoubtedly have appreciated and learned from.

1970

June 4, 1970

Christ understands everything in us. Can I too, in each situation, understand everything? Not to countenance sin, man's entrapment of man, but to grasp all the reasons why. Yes, to go as far as that.

June 6, 1970

It has often been Protestant pastors who have sought to discourage us from making our life commitments. It is true that such commitments were abolished at the Reformation. When certain Catholic sisters or brothers abandon their promises, these pastors cannot keep from exclaiming, "The Reformation was right!" They condemn the ecumenism of a "return to the fold" that some Catholics profess, and yet they themselves practice an ecumenism that says "come and be like us." Fortunately there are other pastors whose generosity knows no bounds.

June 9, 1970

I wonder why, especially on days of relaxation, to entertain myself I let my mind run riot in architectural schemes. My great-grandmother, whom I love without having known her—my sisters and my mother often spoke to me about her—used to fall asleep reorganizing the interior decoration of houses. Transferred to a man's mentality, this means building and construction.

Would she have had the same need to find an escape if she had not been widowed so young? Her husband was a great traveler. He often used to cross the Atlantic in the clippers. Brought down by tuberculosis, he left her with two daughters and two sons. The latter were both to die of the same disease, one at five, the other at twenty.

Perhaps it was these misfortunes that drove her, in her distress, to imagine so many ways of arranging the house. And what about me? Why I am incapable of living somewhere without imagining changes to be made? I estimate distances, in order to take down and always to simplify. It is the same when I read a novel—irresistibly I am led to rewrite it. Often what I read simply provides the outline for a different novel.

June 11, 1970

Here in the house we have abolished all the offices. They turn work into something much too solemn, making a religion of it. We should have nothing but what is really needed for communication.

June 15, 1970

There is a high price to be paid for freedom. Recently some church officials, very generously, wanted to show their support by offering us the means of paying for many of the journeys which young people are making to visit one another across the world. We preferred to refuse these gifts rather than run the risk of losing something of our freedom.

June 22, 1970

Some people, when they are thinking about getting married, come to a decision very quickly. Others opt equally rapidly for celibacy. Is there any reason to think that such people are more mistaken than others who have spent a long time considering everything but who, one fine day, are forced to realize that they have changed in ways they never would have imagined?

June 23, 1970

Summer is in full swing, with vast skies of light. The wind is rising. Darkness is falling across the valley from west to east.

    I surprise myself by the language I use in writing to some young Latin Americans. I know that their commitment for justice springs from love for Christ. Around them men, women, and children are barely aware of their own humanity. A daily nightmare. Oligarchies, often composed of Christians, stifle any capacity they may have for taking control of their own destiny.

I have never been more fully in solidarity with these young Christians, and I write to tell them so. They are preparing for the day when they will take up arms to overthrow tyranny, but they are not seeking their own interests. When the time comes, they will be able to lay them down again. They will refuse to enter into the process by which, once the tyrant is overthrown, all means are justified in the competition to become leaders. I pray with them. Although I know that the gospel in me protests against the use of violence, I am in communion with them, since the violence of oppression is so present in the society in which they live.

June 24, 1970

Robert, as he is about to leave Lima for Cuba, sends me this text, written by a girl belonging to a group of Christian revolutionaries. It is a letter to contemplatives:

"I am writing to those contemplatives who feel deeply concerned by the suffering and the struggles in the world today. In the name of all who are struggling, known or unknown, in the name of all those committed to building a new society, I ask you urgently not to give up your vocation. Find ways of being totally attentive to others, sharing their searching, their successes and their failures, their struggles. Live in the rhythm of people's sorrows and joys, but do not be afraid of doing so in the context of your own particular calling. Seek new forms, by all means, but do not reject what is fundamental in the call you have received from the Lord. The world has need of it, even though it may not realize it or explicitly say so."

June 25, 1970

Visit of a young bishop from northern Italy. The transparence of his heart gives us a hint of what a bishop in Italy will be like in the church of the future. Those most capable of understanding the brand new vitality that is manifesting itself everywhere are also the most ill-used: people have no hesitation in profiting from their openness.

June 26, 1970

This afternoon Bernard, a young man from a nearby village, was ordained priest in the church at St. Gengoux.[23] Since time immemorial no one has been ordained in these parts. I recall the welcome I received from the priest in that same village thirty years ago, the trust he showed me from the first moment. At that time his church was always practically empty; it seemed as though everything had been extinguished forever. He too was giving aid to political refugees. I relive one of our first encounters: Emmanuel Mounier[24] happened to be passing through Taizé, and the two of us cycled over to see him. We were both enthralled: lost in that isolated corner, that priest was full of attention for all that was happening.

July 3, 1970

Some engineers following a refresher course in computer science at Cluny come to share our supper. One of them, an atheist, vigorously contests all that Christians believe. His scientific mind gauges everything by what he can know. At the end of the evening I tell him, "The questions you have been asking are questions that a man living by the certainty of God also dares to keep asking

---

23. St Gengoux-le-National, a small town twelve kilometers to the north of Taizé.

24. Emmanuel Mounier (1905–1950), French personalist philosopher, founder of the journal *Esprit*.

himself his whole life long. This kind of questioning, which is part of a fundamental doubt in us, does not prevent us from constantly setting out from doubt towards believing."

July 7, 1970

Some people, sensing timidity in others, immediately adopt an intimidating approach towards them. But surely it is better not to be feared, even at the risk of fostering forms of pressure or blackmail, rather than to cultivate a distant attitude that only evokes an artificial respect.

July 8, 1970

We have just buried Jean-Christophe Rémy, my sixty-seventh great-nephew. Why the death of this child? For us—unable to understand his death in any way—after a first attack of pitiful grief, a star has come to shine in the darkness.

July 12, 1970

I am still amazed to see the constant floods of young people arriving on the hill. When I came to live at Taizé in 1940, I had no inkling of this. I used to say to my first brothers, "We will stop at twelve brothers. . . ." Later on, when crowds began to come, we thought of moving away. It took laypeople from the region to keep us here. But I would like to remain ignorant as to where we shall die.

July 15, 1970

Tiredness, loss of drive. May this day—may these days—pass quickly! Lassitude and indifference to Christ are one and the same.

Come back to Christ in simple ways. Listen to your own breathing: you share in a life. . . . Listen to the clock striking the hour. . . . Listen to the wind in the lime trees. . . .

July 18, 1970

Max and I went for a walk along the brow of the hill as far as Ameugny.[25] All was enchanting. We said little as we walked. A stroll in shades of blue. To the north, the slopes above St. Gengoux bursting with joy, yellow wheat to give warmth to the blues. Alfalfa just sprouting from the dry, cracked soil. A series of small fields yielding little—vines, potatoes, wheat. Fullness of vast horizons dominated at this time of year by the song of the skylark.

July 23, 1970

Among the children alongside me at the midday prayer is Maria de Fatima. A month ago she and her grandmother crossed the Portuguese border secretly. Her father was killed in Angola. She is often here beside me, praying with her face against the floor.

July 26, 1970

In the mail comes a postcard depicting the front of a church illuminated in the night. On the back a message, "Thank you for the night-light." The child who wrote it was beside me with the other children for several days. Puzzling and uncommunicative. No response until one day, questioning him, I discovered that he was afraid of the dark. At the next service I gave him a night-light to keep in his bedroom while he slept.

All these children close to me each day! If they only knew how much their attentiveness to Christ supports our own!

---

25. Ameugny, a small village close to Taizé on the other flank of the same hill.

1970

July 28, 1970

Four in the morning. Went out for a moment, as I do almost every day at dawn. The star-studded sky is growing pale. A dim dawn begins to break. A month ago, at this hour, the northern sky was transparent, light green, then rapidly ablaze. Now autumn mists are already toning down much of the light's brilliance. In a few hours I shall again be taking the path along the hill as far as the church. I was walking along that same path yesterday evening, pausing to breathe in the night, a burning Eastern night. Today everything is soft and mild again. The distant views are light and peaceful. I am truly restored to the Burgundy of my mother's forebears.

July 29, 1970

Over the last few days, long talks with three young Latin Americans. Yesterday afternoon we found, only a few minutes from here, an unknown and inviting path. I had not realized that the forester's lodge at Praye marked the start of a path through thick woods. Age-old beech trees, carpets of russet leaves.

Pedro—a deep thinker—is preoccupied by what response to give to the revolutionary movement. Carlos is tense to the point of anxiety at the thought that the church moves forward in declarations, lots of words followed by the same emptiness as before. Victor listens. He will soon be back in his country. His desire is to be a simple witness there, nothing else. He is preparing himself for that.

Pedro resumes. If there are no places that offer the possibility of being immersed in a contemplative form of prayer from time to time, how can we avoid being rapidly consumed by ideas? In Latin America, who will maintain a stable presence in places where prayer opens towards a sense of eternity and where there is a listening ear for people of every inclination?

July 30, 1970

Have come up against strong resistance in recent days to the fact that South Americans, young women or men, have such a big place in the preparation of the Council of Youth.

And then yesterday I was told of the presence of a young African bishop here on the hill. I meet him at noon, just before the midday prayer. We sit facing one another. In just a few moments, I realize that it is an exceptional encounter. Yet we have said little. Several others are waiting their turn. We agree to have a meal together. And there I shall persuade him to stay here for a few days.

In the evening we are together in my room. Suddenly he asks me to help him know himself better and, to that end, to question him, so that he may be a man of truth. I agree, but want him to do the same for me. "Do not be afraid to contradict me," he says. I would not be capable of it.

August 2, 1970

Heat pouring down on the countryside. But the nights are cool, incomparably so.

Started to read *Le lys dans la vallée*.[26] I have not opened anything by Balzac since I was fifteen. I recall the long hours of reading aloud as a family. I can see Lily again, the sister whose death came so prematurely, gathering us together during the autumn in father's study and reading a series of works by Balzac to the youngest of us.

How is it that I am carried back still further, to my early childhood, the years when my mother's mother played such a prominent role? I loved her for her calm dignity. She used to live somewhere in Paris, towards the west. Perhaps stories I have quite forgotten lie behind the way I look so poetically westwards and see there a kind of gate to Happiness (and I find myself writing the word with a capital H!).

26. A novel by Honoré de Balzac (1799–1850), realistic and very influential French writer.

During those years of my childhood, it was my grandmother who represented in my eyes all feminine understanding. I have often imagined scenes of high-topped trees, bathed by the setting sun in the midst of broad meadows and there, sitting beneath the foliage, my grandmother and my mother in a welcoming attitude. From them I learned to love spacious country houses. Apparently when I was still only a child I used to say how, one day, I would live in the country and welcome others. I would even plan out the programs for those days, with a lot of time set aside for reading aloud.

Late afternoon. Nothing is more serene than this moment at the end of a hot Sunday. The tireless music of a blowfly. The quiet of my room. Windows shut because of the stifling heat outdoors. The shutters to the south closed as well. All the light enters through the northern window and there I sit to write.

I keep open the door leading onto the stairs of the *salle claire*; coolness comes flooding up from below.

August 3, 1970

The third conversation with Cipriano will remain etched within me. He tells of his two weeks of reflection here. And then he begins to insist that he wants to take what he has experienced here in Taizé and transpose it to his home in Central America. I suggest that he search instead how to enter into the life of his own country, without copying anybody. I conclude by saying, "Forget Taizé!" It makes me unhappy to have to speak like this, but we are about to part for good. The bells are ringing and it is important to find words that will be understood. Forget Taizé: forget us, his friends! It is an inhuman thing to ask and besides, is it even possible? Conversations like this, one after another, are wearing.

August 4, 1970

For the second time today I am about to see a young worker-priest.[27] I was preparing to meet somebody exhausted by struggles and I discover a quiet youth, master of himself, burning with the love that fills him. Clear blue eyes. His features, thickened by physical tiredness, crease at every smile. The face of a man who has become poor in company with those who are victims.

August 5, 1970

The young African bishop of a few days ago has returned after an absence. He wants to be called by his Christian name, Stanislas.[28] He talks about his childhood, the love he has for his family. His father and mother were animists; he is a Christian of the first generation. As a theologian, he constantly refers to Irenaeus:[29] that thinker of the second century was also part of a newly born church.

The night is mild. The breeze passes straight through my room. A walk is calling me. In the deep of night or at the first light of dawn, I shall go to consult the sky: what is the weather going to be?

August 10, 1970

I was brought up in the old traditions, but listening to younger people and sharing in their private struggles rids me of certain reflexes of fear. Without these thousands of young people here on the hill, where would I be now, in spite of my desire to be open?

27. The worker-priest movement in France was a groundbreaking attempt, in the 1940s, to bring the gospel to the working class by priests who were sent to share their living conditions and work alongside them. Often involved in controversy with the hierarchy over political allegiances and questions of lifestyle, the movement encountered many ups and downs in the following years.

28. Stanislas Kaburungu (1935–), bishop of Ngozi, Burundi.

29. Saint Irenaeus (c. 130 – c. 203), originally from Asia Minor, became bishop of Lyons in France. He was one of the most influential theologians of the second century.

1970

August 11, 1970

Christian women ensure continuities; they keep up a living tradition; they share with their children the best of the gospel. We men, with our eagerness to be up-to-date, to live God's today, to achieve something, are liable to ensure nothing but the present and—at times—with such fuss!

August 12, 1970

Martin[30] brings me a drawing at the church with an inscription in his childish writing: "You will never be old." I ask him what he means. He explains, "I will look after you and bring you food to eat." This child here beside me, seven years old, alert and silent. "I will bring you food to eat," words that will console me for a long time.

August 14, 1970

Beneath my window, two doves are perched motionless on the edge of the trough. The water is stale and they hesitate to wash in the usual fashion. But the heat is oppressive and they are drawn irresistibly towards this source of refreshment. They have been there now for a good while, although normally they are lively and nervous. As I write I glance up to watch them, waiting motionless for a storm that refuses to break.

There is not enough time for observation and I begin to envy the poets. Of course there is no question of refusing the enormous pressures of life which make themselves felt day after day, even here in my room. But poetic creation is a way of freedom.

---

30. One of the children of the Portuguese families who emigrated to France in the 1960s and settled in the village of Taizé.

August 19, 1970

All my life I have dreaded the thought of signs that are too great for us. Until now we have been taken at our word. But today Raymond Oliver and his wife came to say goodbye after a stay of ten months at Taizé. Casually, he tells me something he had not even mentioned to his wife:

On the evening of August 16, during the prayer, we were all turned towards the sanctuary of the church. Looking up, he sees, a few yards away from the icon there, the form of a woman holding a child, in a strange light. He blinks his eyes, and asks his wife if she sees anything. The image remains visible until the end of the prayer, but he is the only one who sees it. He supposes that it could be Mary with Jesus, but with his Protestant background, this young American college professor is totally unfamiliar with the Virgin.

He had not even intended mentioning it to me this morning.

August 20, 1970

We only create by drawing on our poverty. I am well-placed to assert this today: it is exactly thirty years ago that I discovered Taizé.

September 2, 1970

Words noted by Elizabeth, who has just left: "If I look back over all the mistakes in my life, it seems that they can be summed up in this way: at times I have left Christ to find other people, and at times I have left other people to find Christ. I never realized that it was myself I had to leave behind."

Giving up others for Christ's sake, washing one's hands of everything to do with today's world; or giving up Christ for the sake of others, in order to make a commitment for greater justice. This kind of alternative tears us apart and dislocates us. Never Christ without other people! Never other people without Christ!

1970

September 6, 1970

I have never been so impatient for winter to come. The wood fire to kindle each morning. Scanning the sky for all the effects of subdued light, the sunset skies, breathtaking in their grandeur.

Went walking in the meadows. Sheep have browsed the grass down to the bare earth. Behind the hedges that keep off the north wind, the flock quietly makes its slow way forward, paying no attention to my presence. At one moment I am surrounded on every side. These plump, placid animals feed with startling feverishness. Their panting breath blends in a single musical note, a cantilena.

September 11, 1970

Today my mother begins her ninety-first year. Where does she find her courage, her capacity to read, to write, to receive guests, to remember faces even of the newest acquaintances? She has the sturdiness of her ancient Burgundian forebears.

September 20, 1970

Today, during the community's council meeting, we spoke of the incomprehensions we would be forced to contend with regarding certain aspects of the preparation of the Council of Youth. Every initiative gives rise to contrary forces. And we are only at the beginning.

September 22, 1970

To have opted for love: that choice opens in a person a wound from which he never recovers.

September 23, 1970

This morning, while I was still asleep, a thought took shape in me, so precise that I noted it down right away: "My friend, tell me at least where you live and I will tell you where I am. You will see, we are not so far apart."

If words can come together this logically, even in sleep, why worry about what to say in public? The lips have simply to follow what has already been formulated within.

October 14, 1970

Lines sent by a young Latin American: "My mind is still restless, worried, and despairing. With an immense hope I ask you to search with us: how to find a light, how to illuminate the Latin American revolution from within, so as to make it radical, dynamic, and aimed at lasting peace."

October 30, 1970

Every day this week I have been talking with a young Italian priest. Why does the turmoil in the church so undermine this man?

In him I have seen holiness from very close at hand. At times I could say nothing more than, "Weep." Once I even went to find a handkerchief for him in a drawer. Weep, because it is not possible to bear such a struggle alone, in stony silence. Face to face with him, I have touched on what it can mean for a man to be abandoned. There exist people of silence who radiate communion. The price they pay is high.

As the days went by, the face of Christ appeared to me in this priest so harrowed by his struggles. The depth of his gaze could conceal nothing of his successive ordeals. He has shown me the heart of one of the greatest mysteries: the gift of a whole existence for other people, at the risk of losing all of oneself.

Before parting, after so many days of closeness, I knelt for him to bless me. He could see that I did not wish him to do likewise.

1970

October 31, 1970

A quite extraordinary sunset. The countryside ablaze and, between the flames, fissures of gold and pale green.

November 1, 1970

I love my room with its peach-colored walls, the floor of wide pine planks, and the ceiling of painted beams. Some of us have a larger room, others a smaller one. Some sleep on a mattress laid on the floor and have nothing but a table and a cupboard; others prefer to have more color around them. For each of us, once the door is shut, the same solitude is there waiting. Of course there is the kitchen where we can find others around eleven in the evening, to talk and hear what is happening. Then each returns to his room and closes the door. Our lifelong yes to Christ means taking this step every evening. Sometimes it is costly. But this solitude is not in order to seek one's own self. . . . As the years pass, it opens us to the one Reality—Christ, our first love.

November 2, 1970

Waking up in the night, I read a few pages of Victor Chklovski's *Tolstoy*.[31] After I put out the light, my mind remains fixed on Tolstoy and Yasnaya Polyana. To think that his daughter is still alive and could tell so much! An hour of joy in the presence of a fascinating Russia!

November 3, 1970

Deeply affected as a small child by my parents' great worries, I would make them mine and be tormented by them. I became aware of life, a large family, a father so anxious to provide for everything.

---

31. Victor Chklovski, *Léon Tolstoï*, Vol. 1. 1828–1870 (Paris: Gallimard, 1969); Vol 2. 1870–1910 (Paris: Gallimard, 1970).

It was at that time, so as not to add to my parents' burdens, that I got into the habit of not telling them of my own difficulties. Still today, afraid of overburdening my brothers with my cares, I keep silences which must, in fact, be hard for them.

November 17, 1970

Days marked by the presence of a young man from Mexico. In his view, the faithful church is always on the outskirts of society, contesting it, denouncing oppressive authorities, the power of wealth, privileges. It sets itself in a situation of weakness. To interpret events, it sees as those who are oppressed see.

November 20, 1970

Another Mexican at our table. I tell him how, three days ago, his place was occupied by a young revolutionary from his country. My brothers are astonished: so he was a revolutionary, that young man who, in great simplicity, shared with us his conviction that the evangelization of the Mexican people was made possible thanks to the Virgin who appeared to a poor man in the sixteenth century. The likeness of the Virgin, with Indian features, left its imprint on the man's cloak and the attention of the masses has remained centered on that sign for the past four hundred years.

November 21, 1970

Words of a little girl who lost her mother a few years ago: "When you own a lot of things, you are rich, but when you do not have all that, perhaps you are rich in love."

November 22, 1970

The past interests me less and less. What lies ahead I view in an optimistic light.

November 23, 1970

Woken in the night by a racket: mice gallivanting about more riotously than ever. I seem to feel the breath of one of them on my cheek. No, they have never been that bold. And suddenly I sense a weight on my blankets. I turn on the light, and see before me a huge sewer rat. I leap out of bed and see that my wrist is scratched and bleeding. I realize that this is the daily lot of so many badly housed people.

November 24, 1970

A few years ago an economist, a nonbeliever, to whom I spoke about some conversations I was about to have with certain church leaders, said to me, "These conversations about money and power in the church will crush you; people crash against the wall of money." The talks took place and, as he predicted, they were a complete failure . . . but that does not mean I am done for.

November 25, 1970

Consent to the fact that we are living in a pre-revolutionary time, where relationships are expressed through criticism and conflict. But know how to gain inner perspective when criticism resorts to polemics or blackmail. Christians can never equate needful criticism with contempt for persons.

December 3, 1970

At Rome since Sunday. Yesterday, Charles-Eugène, Bruno,[32] and I decided to take the train for Eboli. The carriage is full of young

---

32. Brother Charles-Eugène (Magnin, 1938–), Swiss, longtime secretary to Brother Roger who, after his death, was instrumental in publishing his collected writings in French. Brother Bruno (Toedtli, 1940–), Swiss German, for many years has lived with the *fraternité* of brothers in Brazil. He was ordained a priest in 1980 by the bishop of Alagoinhas to help with the pastoral needs of

people, as well as women from southern Italy, each fascinated by the sound of her own voice. It is a matter of who can talk in the most demonstrative way. The train speeds along. The warm air billows in through the corridor windows.

Leaving the train, we find a car for hire that will take us up to the mountain villages. And before long we are at Eboli, where Carlo Levi, in one of his novels, tells how "Christ stopped at Eboli."[33] After which there was nothing but ruin and misery. We speed on along the foot of the mountain, through high-grown meadows. Roads lined with olive trees, with leafy and yellowed plane trees. Then the car plunges into a narrow, sunless gorge. And in a flash we see before us, perched on one side of the valley, the town of Campagna.

The car comes to a halt in a square, at the foot of a high, white palazzo. We continue on foot, climbing up and down narrow alleyways alive with children.

In a large room illuminated through the open door, a man is weaving chair seats out of straw. He talks to us about his life. When it is cold, he lights a fire in a corner of the room. The smoke climbs up beneath the soot-stained vault and escapes through a small opening. He claims to be old. When still in the prime of life, he spent seven years working in Germany. His eyes glint with a green light. His toothless smile and drawn features can conceal nothing of the struggles making up his life. The more he tries to explain his existence here, the more I am struck by the contained fervor, the contemplative vigor that are his. No, Christ did not stop at Eboli; he is here and this man is, without realizing it, a witness to him. I want to tell him so, but something holds me back. For the rest of the afternoon his face haunts me. Why did we not dare tell him we were Christians, and that in his house we encountered the one we are looking for?

---

that poor Brazilian diocese.

33. Carlo Levi (1902–1975), Jewish writer and doctor from Turin active in the anti-Fascist movement between the two world wars. Author of the well-known book of that title telling of his forced exile in the South of Italy in the 1930s.

1970

At the town's highest point we join a crowd. Leaning against the walls of a house are palm wreaths interwoven with carnations, ready to be carried to the church. Women and children are entering and leaving the home of the deceased through a vaulted entrance. The women are visibly afflicted; one still has tears on the edge of her upper lip. Most are wearing aprons. A gleaming coffin emerges from the house. Only the men of the family follow the widower. The dignity of the sons is in tune with the respect of the crowd.

As we walk down we are invited, as we were on the way up, to enter various houses. We do not dare to, except for one tiny kitchen full of a dozen children. On the table a loaf of bread, three-quarters eaten. The excitement of the children as we pass.

Leaving Campagna, we drive on towards Valva. The hills are planted with ancient, towering oaks. Sometimes a huge pig attached to a tree scratches after the fallen acorns. Elsewhere an old man gathers more acorns along the edge of the road. We cross the valley. Before us rises the mountain. A land of old men, which clings to the rocks. All is slowly dying. In one village the bell is tolling. Another funeral. We enter the church, whose sanctuary is built out on foundations descending to the foot of the ravine. In the church there is a little group gathered around the coffin— a father, his sons, a few women. In the street, all the doors are already shut. A youth is carrying wood. He invites us to enter his home. Before the flames on the hearth a young woman is bent down, stirring the pasta. An old couple, and two tiny children. They invite us to stay and eat.

At Valva, thick mists still reflect some glimmers of daylight. Two women come down the street bearing bundles on their heads. With them is a stout, rotund peasant, with a big smile on his face. When he speaks, there is no mistaking the cheerfulness of his tone. The women are laughing at the sight of a sheepskin sticking out from beneath his jacket. An old couple watch us from a terrace high up. They gesture to us to come up to their home—too small a house, the husband maintains. His wife, bent with age, seems more like his mother. They insist on offering us coffee. The old man leads us behind a curtain so that we can see their large modern bed. Everything is gleaming and fresh, as he repeats, "Too small."

December 4, 1970

Yesterday Thomas[34] joined us after a month in England. To celebrate his arrival we climbed to the top of the Pincio.[35] The city is already plunged in shadow. Irresistibly our talk turns to Taizé.

One of the brothers mentions a comment made by my sister Genevieve about our first years at Taizé: "It was a terribly bleak time." It was wartime. Those we were housing were hunted people, on the run. And then certain people in the area, anxious to keep out of trouble with the authorities, took measures against us which could have had serious consequences. A written accusation was drawn up against Genevieve and the worst could have happened.

It was at that time that I discovered just what people are capable of towards their fellows. I can situate the exact moment of that discovery. When I learned the inconceivable, I was at the foot of the woods. I went back to the house and on the stairway beside my room I stopped, frozen with horror. I knew that I would never at any time seek to take revenge.

I write this twenty-four hours after having spoken of it in order to unburden myself.

December 6, 1970

Quiet morning alone. I read letters, almost all of them written by young people. They are a bath of life. In them I find the inner struggles of my own youth. But I also discern a refusal to settle down, not at all customary thirty years ago.

---

34. Brother Thomas (Ian Williamson, 1939–2019), from Scotland.
35. One of the seven hills of Rome.

1970

December 7, 1970

Re-read a letter which Daniel[36] sent to me at Rome some years ago, in which he tells of a dream he had:

"We are in the Vatican, at the very top of a many-storied building, at a papal audience. The room is crowded and we are close to Paul VI. The pope, consumed with worry, has collapsed on to a simple chair. Meanwhile a priest, apparently the spokesman for the Holy Father, is addressing words to the crowd, against which the pope attempts in vain to protest. At this moment you intervene, scandalized at this abuse of power, but not for long. We hear the cries of a group of pilgrims under whom the flooring, which is quite rotten, is giving way. In a flash, all the planking dissolves into dust. We and the Holy Father remain balanced on a beam until an obliging person places a ladder—too short but nonetheless effective—that allows us to climb down to the foot of the building, where we find a crowded market in progress."

And this brother adds this commentary to his dream: "So I suppose the situation in the church troubles us even in our nights! The church, well hidden in and around us . . . of no great appearance, but within, what fire."

December 11, 1970

Very often, in spite of ourselves, our ordeals, failures, and standstills constitute a driving force stimulating us to create, to such an extent that the impossible becomes the way towards the possible.

December 21, 1970

Return to Taizé. There I find these lines written by a young man: "To be free means knowing that you are in chains, and still setting out; knowing that you are going to fall, and still standing up. But

---

36. Daniel de Montmollin (1921–), Swiss, one of the first four brothers, who began the pottery workshop in Taizé and enjoyed international renown as a potter.

it is hard.... Nonetheless I keep at it; I try to hang on and always end up falling down again. It involves a fight. I want to prepare the Council of Youth but I must have festival within myself to begin with."

December 22, 1970

In Paris to pray beside the mortal remains of Pastor Boegner.[37] The coffin is exposed in his drawing room. Before closing it, the family placed in it his Bible and the Taizé office, which he used to pray daily.

At midday, the light is dazzling. Huge clouds loom over the buildings. We take a taxi driven by an elderly woman. As we cross the Seine, we talk to her about the light. Today the days begin to grow longer. I marvel at all I see—a sky, the decorated streets, all that can be read in people's faces.

December 28, 1970

Today the prisoners of the Burgos trial were condemned to death.[38] This evening I sent General Franco this telegram, prepared with young people: "In the name of human dignity, pardon the Burgos prisoners. In every person God is present. Do not wound the consciences of the young. It is with many of them that we make this appeal."

---

37. Marc Boegner (1881–1970), French pastor, former president of the Reformed Church of France and of the Protestant Federation of France, a friend of the Taizé Community from the beginning.

38. During the dictatorial regime of General Francisco Franco in Spain, nine of the sixteen Basque nationalists on trial in Burgos for an attack against a Spanish policeman were condemned to death. Local and international pressure was successful in commuting the death penalty to a prison sentence.

December 29, 1970

Just before Christmas, three young people returned from Spain. They had been there for a month and they told their stories with unsmiling faces. There are narratives that discourage, but do not lead to despair. Today, after the midday prayer, we shared a meal to celebrate their return. Festivity in the heart of struggle. Festivity around a meal. A small community poised in expectation, knowing the importance of a presence hidden in our midst. All the meals that Christians have shared for the last two thousand years passed before my eyes. A time of sharing, simplicity of heart, and we are ready to face new combats.

1971

Brother Roger's journal for 1971 continues the topics of the previous year: talks with young people concerned with greater justice in society, contacts with Christians notably from Latin America and Africa, reflections on nature and life in the countryside. There is perhaps a greater emphasis on events in the region of Taizé, for example the arrival of a family of Portuguese immigrants. The prior of Taizé also crosses the Atlantic, visiting New York to speak to the bishops of the Episcopal Church in the United States, and at the end of the year makes his customary visit to Rome, where a synod of bishops has just taken place. There he reflects on the question of the ministry and priestly celibacy, and has an important private audience with Pope Paul VI.

January 1, 1971

Two hours spent passing from one group to another, from one individual to another. An immense variety of aspirations. Are we going to see an acceleration of the present atomizing process in the years to come? Those who are youngest give reasons for thinking so.

Try and understand, again and again, without getting upset if some of them use rough language. Let go of certain mental structures. Universalize one's comprehension.

January 4, 1971

Three days of conversations with Italian workers involved in union activities. Sergio analyzes the church harshly. I wonder whether, like many others, he is going to say that it is on the point of dying. But his conclusion is: "The church, dead? Oh no, the church is constantly moving forward."

In his opinion, it is essential to criticize the church's structures because that sets us free; it is a way of getting rid of all that we cannot bear, in order to have room to live. Without such criticism the only way left would be to reject the church as a whole. Creating awareness in people and criticizing help us pass from simple refusal to creative initiatives.

The uncompromising passion for the church, for the People of God, in this union worker, is quite typical of a young Italian. How can we not discern in it a sign of love?

January 5, 1971

Two Christmas messages strike me particularly.

A card bearing an image of Christ with a rifle. The message is full of friendship towards us but harsh in its language: "People are not dogs, enough of that. But we will change things. Man no longer to be wolf for man. A challenge: hope and fight. Christ didn't rise for nothing. Meeting place Taizé, Easter."

And a letter from young Spaniards who are living together in a small community. I find, on seeing the letterhead on their writing paper, that they have given my own name to their endeavor. I immediately write to them to tell them not to do so.

January 7, 1971

The fire, constantly stoked during the day, is burning this evening on a bed of glowing embers. Beyond the windows snow sparkles, hardened by the frost. In my room Alain and I listen to the concerto in C minor for two harpsichords and orchestra by J. S. Bach. More than our words, certain passages of the concerto communicate a wealth of gladness. Over twenty years of the same unblemished trust. . . .

January 8, 1971

Aware of all one's thoughts, afraid of none. . . .

January 10, 1971

This Sunday is one of the few in the year with no meetings. I was not expecting to see anybody and, one after another, a whole series of unexpected visitors arrived. One was a young South American. He bears in him a treasure of faith lived generation after generation, but he is also hesitant. Is he going to be the rich young man of the gospel, generous but indecisive, or the man who, in spite of everything, will commit himself irrevocably? At the door I repeat: seek Christ, not secondarily but as your first love and therefore, here and now, as your essential joy. I sense in him the sadness of the man who longs. . . . Will he make it?

January 15, 1971

Day of shadows, André Thurian[1] is dying of cancer. We are the same age. On the telephone, his aged mother, eighty-five years old—a poor, broken voice in the twilight of her life.

And in the mail a letter from Peter Rutishauser.[2] He informs me of the result of his operation: a malignant tumor. All he asks for is a few more years to work.

It is easier to consent to our own death than to that of those who are close to us. Rational explanations are no help.

January 20, 1971

Visit to the stable. Our three cows are chewing the cud, completely indifferent. Only the goat lifts an inquisitive head. Visit to the village church. Return to the house. Down in the valley a frog is croaking, the first sign of the coming spring.

January 22, 1971

Suppose that, overwrought because of our consumer society, we were to react against it to the point of rejecting technological developments? Technological civilization is not at fault; in itself it is neutral. Everything depends on the way it is used. It can be a motive force to set people free, offering the means to deliver them from subjection to the elements—floods, epidemics. . . . It allows agriculture and medicine to progress . . . as never before.

Any civilization carries its attendant dangers. But whatever the civilization may be, Christ is there, close to us, and today he is close to us as we try, with new sciences, to bring something of the creation into a new harmony.

---

1. The elder brother of Brother Max.

2. Peter Rutishauser, a psychoanalyst from Zurich who came to Taizé in 1968 for a silent retreat. Deeply impressed by his outlook, Brother Roger continued the relationship and encouraged several brothers to speak with him until his death in 1972. See *Brother Roger's Journals*, 1:114.

1971

January 23, 1971

Visit from the Anglican bishop Oliver Tomkins. He was the only priest present when the first brothers made their life commitment in 1949. At today's meal we talked of the ground covered since, of our impressions.

He was also at Taizé for the inauguration of the church on August 6, 1962. Would we ever dream of inaugurating a building today? I would like to see our church sunk beneath the ground, buried in the depths like a catacomb. Eight meters high, it already seems like a relic from another age.[3]

During our meal, my eyes wandered over the countryside stretching beyond the three windows of the room. The plowed fields, studded with large puddles, glistened beneath the lowering sky. Certain twigs, red with the first rising sap, hinted that spring will soon break through. Beside the clock a vase of yellow jasmine, picked this very morning.

January 26, 1971

Letter from a Christian living in a nearby village: I would like you to know "how much, in our vineyards of Macon, we need you . . ." If I note down these lines, that is because they come from our own soil, a soil that has been stony for centuries.

January 28, 1971

At noon on the organ, a piece by Bach in the style of *The Art of Fugue*. In the permanent struggle that has to be fought for Christ's sake with men of clear-cut temperament, such moments of surrender are like a quenching dew.

Night has fallen. Every evening at this hour I glimpse the light shining in the window where two women of prayer live, both

---

3. And yet that church was already becoming too small for the crowds that were flocking to Taizé, so that it had to be enlarged by circus tents and, later on, by permanent structures. See *Brother Roger's Journals*, 1:62.

of them elderly.[4] No one will ever know all that their presence has meant. Today the window is in darkness. They must be away. An emptiness in the night.

February 1, 1971

This afternoon José[5] lit the bread oven in the kitchen. After the evening prayer, it only took a few bits of wood for me to kindle it again. Above the embers a dull flame rose up into the chimney. Later in the evening, the oven emitted the odor of the bundle of kindling placed there, ready to be lit tomorrow morning.

February 2, 1971

Two doves are cooing in a room nearby. We managed to find them late last night at Paul Deschaume's farm. In a few moments I am going to carry them to the church for the celebration of the Eucharist and I am eager to enjoy everyone's surprise. This is the day when Mary presents the Child in the temple with the offering of a poor family—a pair of doves.

February 23, 1971

Shrove Tuesday. We have invited people from the area to an evening meal. The elderly ones possess a dignity which says much about the culture transmitted through centuries of rural life.

---

4. Since 1963, two of the first members of the Grandchamp Community, Sister Marguerite de Beaumont (1895–1986) and Sister Gilberte de Rougemont (1904–1993), were living in the village of Taizé. Grandchamp is an ecumenical monastic community of women in Switzerland begun in the Reformed Church in the 1930s. Brother Roger drew inspiration from the sisters of Grandchamp while searching for his own vocation, and they later adopted the Rule of Taizé.

5. Brother José (Corominas, 1909–1994), originally from Barcelona.

1971

March 29, 1971

A year ago today the Council of Youth was announced. This year we were not expecting very many more young people for Easter, but over six thousand are already registered. We are obliged to tear down part of the facade of the church and extend it by a huge circus tent. The decision, taken rapidly, was not easy. What lies before us will require a flexibility and adaptability of which as yet we have no idea.

April 14, 1971

Meeting with a group from Toulouse. Suddenly I recall a journey back from Toulouse in the night. I think that it was during the winter of 1966. That evening, speaking in a gymnasium, I had been obliged to climb into a boxing ring. In the night train, once alone, I kept repeating to myself: Roger, this evening must be the last; you must never again agree to speak to such crowds. I was forgetting that we are led by Another, often in directions we would not have wished to go.[6]

April 24, 1971

Eight children between ten and twelve years of age have arrived. They are children of miners at Montceau[7] who managed to find somebody to drive them over. They will stay until Monday to help welcome visitors. At each service they are there, kneeling in single file.

At home, on Fridays they go to their local church and pray, without anyone ever having suggested this to them.

What if the springtime of the church were being made present in the faces of children and old people from whom nothing is expected? Suppose they have received the spirit of prophecy?

---

6. See John 21:18.

7. Montceau-les-Mines, a mining town forty kilometers from Taizé. One of the first *fraternités* of brothers lived there in the 1950s.

What these eight children have spontaneously undertaken is so unexpected! Talking with them, I was fascinated by their attitude, stamped with a kind of seriousness.

April 26, 1971

With several of my brothers I have been to visit Marcel Buisson, the priest of Culles-les-Roches.[8] He is eighty-five. His face, still smooth, beams with happiness. An electric bulb over the table lights the room. The shutters are half-open: since his heart attack he cannot make the effort necessary to open them completely.

"I became a priest very late," he tells us. "They were against ordaining me. I was sick with scruples. It was a real sickness, fearing sin in everything. I never knew joy. The priest who prepared me for the priesthood assured me that I might know joy only at the very end. So I wait."

At the back of the room, in a recess, is a plank from a confessional. Would he agree to some of us coming to receive absolution at his hands? "There are better priests," he replies, giving names. And he adds, "I have been in this village for forty years, but nothing has happened." He spoke like this when I came to see him before. Like so many others, he does not believe that what he achieves can have any impact.

April 29, 1971

Yesterday evening two brothers returned from Spain. In Avila they arrived, unannounced, at the Carmelite convent. The sister at the gate welcomed them without surprise, firing as her first question: "How is Brother Roger?" Every day without exception, that community prays for us. I understand how it is that we hold firm.

---

8. Culles-les-Roches, a village twenty kilometers from Taizé.

1971

April 30, 1971

Every evening these days, I am drawn towards the north to see the last gleams of light, to make out dimly the long ridges of the hills dipping down beyond St. Gengoux. It is eleven o'clock. In the distance, many glimmering lights join in a dance. What is this performance, isolated as we are here in the midst of poor, practically unlit villages?

May 10, 1971

Gave *Ta fête soit sans fin*[9] to be printed. Of all the pages written day after day in the last two years, which ones to choose? When I finally lay the pen down, the question arises: have I managed to say what I wanted to? No. Then why write? There is always a limit that remains, beyond which we are left alone with ourselves, whether we are writing or speaking spontaneously.

May 13, 1971

Denis[10] has an aged aunt who wrote to him just after her eighty-fifth birthday, "Very often I glimpse Christ, as you see someone around the house, not really seeing him, and yet seeing him." She lives alone in a farmhouse high up in the Jura Mountains.

May 23, 1971

At table, Edouard Gafaringa, a young African pastor from Remera in Rwanda. A man of openness and friendship. I begin by saying, "You are here to see children." A look of astonishment. "After all,

---

9. Brother Roger's journal from 1969 to 1970, published as the first part of this book.

10. Brother Denis (Jean-Daniel Aubert, 1934–2015), originally from French-speaking Switzerland. An architect by training, he designed the Church of Reconciliation; he spent many years in Africa as the brother in charge of the *fraternités* in Nairobi (Kenya) and Senegal.

are we anything but children?" A burst of laughter. As we part, he tells of his longing to go and live, with his wife and family, near my brothers in Kigali.[11]

May 30, 1971

A brother, back from a journey to a country whose name is best not mentioned, tells of all that is being prepared there for the Council of Youth. Even if we lived solely for the Christians of that land, existence would already have a meaning for us.[12]

June 4, 1971

Splendor of my room in the early working hours. A warm light, objects clearly defined, the coolness of the air scarcely warmed since the night. We go to the far ends of the earth in search of what is offered close at hand.

June 12, 1971

Have welcomed all week at our table Massarou, a young man from Japan. In order to become a Christian, he was first obliged to adopt the concepts and thought patterns of the Western world. That was the way the missionaries wanted it. He only began to grasp the Gospel once he had freed himself from Western categories. So I told him, "Preside at the table, take my place here and welcome us; we are your prodigal sons, Westerners as your missionaries were." Massarou begin to preside with incredible joy and tact.

---

11. A small group of brothers lived in Kigali, the capital of Rwanda, from 1966 to 1972.

12. From 1962 on, brothers made discreet visits to support Christians in the Communist countries of Eastern Europe: East Germany, Czechoslovakia, Hungary, Romania, Poland, and the Soviet Union.

June 14, 1971

In the plane from Paris to New York, in response to an invitation from the American bishops of the Anglican Communion. The happiness of a child. How I have danced for joy these past few days at the thought of crossing the ocean! America: a childhood dream. The stories of my great-grandfather. Since then, an undying nostalgia for the wide open spaces, a land without borders.

June 15, 1971

Meeting with the bishops. They asked me to speak to them about authority in the church, and also of the ministry of the Pope.

Where does this inner calm come from, this absence of timidity? Only ten years ago, I never dared to speak in public, even in the church at Taizé. I remember that in August 1962, during the days our church was inaugurated, I did not pronounce a single word in public.

June 16, 1971

Even in New York, I lose none of my rural habits. At around four in the morning I leap out of bed to see what the weather will be like. But the sky is still dark, whereas at Taizé, once three is past, it begins to change color and take my breath away with outbursts of new light.

At about six, I go to the kitchen and find Beatrice, an old Brazilian woman, tiny and plump, walking with difficulty. Her existence is rife with the harshest ordeals, humiliation and desertion. She is bursting with kindness. All her life long she has tried to give love.

June 17, 1971

Yesterday the assembly of bishops was impressive by its attentiveness. While speaking, struck by their concentration, I included moments of silence. Such moments are necessary, pauses to catch one's breath. But through them I also find that I can sense whether or not my words really stimulate reflection. Those silences taught me much. I had been unaware of the quality of these Anglican bishops. It is not for nothing that they are descendants of the pioneers who set out westwards.

In between the meetings, I try to discover the futuristic side of New York. Nothing is more impressive than the great towering buildings. Disappointed at so much uniformity and monotony. And the youth is not so very different from that of Europe.

June 18, 1971

During the whole of my stay in New York, I did not speak a single word in English. Could it be because of some words my father used to repeat years ago, "One does not speak a foreign language to grate on other people's ears"?

But sitting beside the driver in a taxi, I dared tell him in English how happy I was to see men and women from both the Northern and the Southern continents in New York. In spite of all the present conflicts, could there be here an anticipation of the humanity of the future? He does not contradict me, and I even sense in him a tacit agreement.

Now we are flying over Ireland. In the central aisle of the plane a young mother is standing with a tiny baby in her arms. The child's head, resting on its mother's shoulder, is rolling from side to side. In him, all the children of the whole world are present. His mother is tirelessly stroking his back, as though by that gesture she were giving him life.

As we left this morning, Beatrice was radiant. In the meantime I had learned more of her story. Two years ago she had an operation for cancer. At that time she used to say, "It is good that

God has chosen me, because I know how to suffer." As we parted, I kissed the hands of this old Brazilian cook, saying, "I want to kiss the hands of a saint." "Don't say that," she replied. "it's a heresy. Call me a missionary." To which I answered, "A saint is nothing other than a witness to Jesus Christ and you are that more than many others." Her eyes filled with tears. Her brow was dark, almost black, marked by cobalt treatment. And I added, "We shall pray together for the leaders of the church, for them not to be afraid of the future any longer, and even less afraid of young people." I heard her reply, "With young people, it is never any good pulling on the leash to make them comply; the only thing that counts is kindness."

June 27, 1971

A new family of Portuguese immigrants has just arrived at Taizé: Antonio, his wife, their four youngest children, and their son-in-law Francisco. Two days and two nights by train. A definitive departure from their native land in order to come and settle here. Francisco returned ill from Angola.[13] Twenty-four years old, he is as gaunt as a skeleton. Soon he will be followed by his wife and children. We and these families will live close to one another at Taizé. How can we achieve a relationship of sharing without patronizing them? Since my journey last winter to Paços de Ferreira, their village, that question has been haunting me. For so many migrants, exile means a lessening of their humanity.

July 3, 1971

When I ask the children kneeling by my side whom we should pray for, they frequently reply: for Jesus, for God. Could it be that they are so aware of the free gifts of God that they consider any other request to be superfluous?

---

13. At that time the Portuguese dictatorship was waging a war against fighters for independence in Angola.

The seriousness of the three little Portuguese girls who arrived last week is a sign of their parents' situation. To help the family remain free towards us, I would like to be able to tell them to space out their visits to the church. But I fear I might wound something in them. They alone know why they come to share in our community prayer.

July 7, 1971

A friend, a physicist, asked me recently: how do you manage to organize so many meetings without bureaucracy or ticket windows? If he only knew the constant revising it demands! He also had this to say: as his authority increased and his audience grew, Christ unsettled people in power, Jews and Romans. That is something they cannot forgive. They panic and set to work to provoke his failure. At such moments the masochists appear: "Happy are those who are defeated." They are pessimistic regarding any vaguely new burst of life.

July 16, 1971

The press hints at new relationships between the Western countries and China. Alone in the woods, I sing.

July 26, 1971

Long conversations with a young Latin American bishop.[14] He is going to spend the summer with us. What is to be feared in his country is not the imprisonment and torture of young Christians. Without knowing it, those responsible for these acts oblige the Christians to come to grips with their own identity and prevent them from identifying the church with a political system. The

---

14. Dom Luis Gonzaga Fernandes (1926–2003), auxiliary bishop of Vitoria, Brazil. In 1972, the Taizé brothers who were in Recife moved to live in that city for six years. He was very close to them during that time.

problem lies within the church. It lies in the uncontrollable loss of heart among young priests or young laypeople, often the very best of them. They have gone as far as they could, and have finally left the church forever. "I weep," he says. "I weep whenever another weeps. I inherited that from my father." I interrupt, "Without that inheritance, you would be completely overwhelmed and crushed."

July 28, 1971

To a young man from Central America, I found myself once more insisting that I do not intend to give advice, that each of us has to find our way forward starting from our own human poverty, that he must not look for a "spirit of Taizé." Somewhat impetuously, not to say violently, he retorted, "It is already a spirit not to want there to be one."

August 4, 1971

At the end of the morning, just thirty-five minutes remained to see seven different people.

Henri, a young Frenchman just back from Portugal, tells of a tense moment on his journey. He and his fiancée were almost killed when a munitions dump exploded. The town was full of terror; a grenade skimmed past his face. Then he gives me an olive branch that he received from a Portuguese boy, about to leave for the war in Angola, who explained, "I shall never be a soldier. My trade is looking after olive trees—the tree of peace. I really never thought that I would be using a rifle. Today I'm leaving for Africa. I am a man dressed as a soldier but remember that, whatever happens, I shall remain a human being."

After Henri comes Helder, a boy of eighteen from Portugal. I invite him to lunch tomorrow with the other Portuguese: José, Antonio, Fernando, Manuel. What can we accomplish together?

I have to be quick. There are others to see. I can hear the laughter of newlyweds waiting. But I remain absorbed by the thought of all those men dressed as soldiers, leaving their land for an impossible cause.

August 5, 1971

Meal with the five from Portugal. At once the question burning within me surfaced. Thirty years ago it was wartime and I was living here surrounded by victims of Nazism. So I ask myself: could I today be keeping the kind of silence that at the time I condemned in Christians who refused to take a clear stand? The meal was deadly serious and I was sorry for that. I would have liked there to have been a note of festivity. But to no avail.

August 6, 1971

Stanislas is back! And with him all Africa, with its exuberant quickness of heart. Just before he set out for Europe he had an experience which I noted down as he was relating it. He went to visit a community of African sisters and as bishop, he was to receive the perpetual vows of some of them. He asked them if they grasped all that celibacy entails. They gave this reply: if the church were to say that it no longer makes any sense to believe in the risen Christ, then we would have nothing left but suicide. If Jesus Christ is not risen, there is no point in committing our lives.

August 7, 1971

Telephone call from the Vatican. On Monday the *Osservatore Romano* will announce that "henceforth there is to be a representative of the Prior of Taizé at the Holy See."

At once I went out to walk in the garden alone. The heavy rain of the night was steaming up, warmed by the sun-gorged earth.

Who are you in this event? I see myself, a poor man walking on the uncut grass. For the moment I cannot assess the full significance of this agreement signed three weeks ago. But there is one thing I do know: I love that "pilgrim church that is at Rome" and its bishop. What can I ask of him? Surely to give us light, to warm us with a fire, to stimulate communion among all the churches....

August 8, 1971

About yesterday's event, I knew it was coming. I had thought that perhaps the demands I expressed about the ministry of the pope, at the conference of Pax Romana in July, would hold things up. But not at all. To have a representative close to the pope: not that it means any lessening in the effort to find a more intense communion with the Bishop of Rome.

August 9, 1971

Many conversations, far into the evening. Dire situations, some without any apparent issue. As a result I lie awake in the night. Impossible to digest so much human distress. Lying on my bed and lifting a corner of the window curtain, I discover the garden flooded with moonlight. I go out and walk along the hill as far as the hermitages. In the distance, in the middle of the night, some people are singing in Italian. The air is poised, motionless.

August 10, 1971

A specialist in Chinese tells me that in Chinese the word crisis is composed of two signs: one stands for catastrophe and the other for hope.

August 11, 1971

In Northern Ireland a section of humanity, deprived of basic rights for centuries, feels that it is being deliberately oppressed. Recent events[15] oblige us to ask what we can do to bring peace in such a prolonged conflict. And then yesterday young Irish people who came here repeated what they had already told us a year ago, "Do not come for the moment. It is up to us to act here where we live."

August 15, 1971

After the midday meal, Dom Luis left us. We got up from the table and his eyes were brimming with tears. For my part I was holding my emotions in check, as I learned to do as a child. We never wept in the presence of other people. But once alone, who will ever know?

Luis would like us to spend two months living together in a Latin American *favela*. But how can I tear myself away from here? Any prolonged absence means a return that is inhumanly overburdened. But since my five days in New York I am yearning to cross the ocean again.

August 16, 1971

Declined to see several journalists and television reporters from various countries. Nobody can tackle too many things at once and to receive them at present would be an excessive burden. But it is not fair towards newsmen and -women who do their work with great honesty.

---

15. August 11 was the third and last day of the "Ballymurphy massacre" during which eleven civilians were killed in the course of an operation undertaken by the British "Parachute Regiment" in Northern Ireland and ostensibly directed against the IRA. In the previous two years, the conflict worsened in that region between a nationalistic minority, generally of Irish origin and mainly Catholic, and the "Unionist" majority wishing to remain part of the United Kingdom, who were Protestants and often descended from English or Scottish settlers.

1971

August 17, 1971

With the approach of the Council of Youth, I cannot bring myself to worry, even when some people emphasize the great difficulties involved. I have confidence in the intuitions of the young people from so many different countries who gather here, go home to search and pray, then come back again. In these hot August nights, there are evenings when I find myself out walking beneath a sky laden with stars, at the same time as thousands of young people are camping on the hill. And I tell myself: the innumerable intuitions of these young people are like points of light in my night. As yet nothing is perceptible, and yet my night is festive, aflame and full of an extravagant hope. The future, young people—the two are one. No, I am not anxious about the future. A springtime of the church is at hand. Soon it will be a fire giving us warmth.

August 18, 1971

A blowfly is buzzing in the thick midday heat. All of a sudden, my childhood comes back to me in a burst of joy. I listen to the other noises, light and distant—the trickle of water flowing into the trough, someone's footsteps on the path. The dry-stone wall sheltering the garden is bursting with well-being beneath the clinging vines.

August 19, 1971

Dreamed that the house in which I was born was in flames. I was left with another one, less loved. I felt shocked and hurt. I comforted myself with the thought that an insurance policy would pay for the furnishings, but the letters were going to vanish forever....

August 24, 1971

Visit from a foreign bishop. I wanted to hear what he had to say, but his young vicar-general kept bombarding me with remarks and questions. As soon as he arrived, he had been anxious to let me hear some not very kind words spoken by a Protestant minister—competitive ecumenism at its worst. Dismayed, I try to turn to other subjects. No good. Twice, in an attempt to reply to his indiscreet questions, I give him texts to read. But he keeps it up, while the bishop remains silent. Finally I invite my visitors to read the texts in silence, and I put on a record of Valentini's trumpet concerto in C major. It is the first time I have had to avail myself of that method as a way of putting an end to such nonsense!

August 26, 1971

Wrote to Michel[16] at Recife: "If the pen were able to express our communion, I would need to write to you in letters of flame." In the midst of all the contradictions in which we are set by our vocation, this brother's courage bears me onward.

August 27, 1971

At this hour of the afternoon, a ray of sunlight is entering through the half-open shutters and flooding the two pages of the atlas open on regions in the far north of Siberia and Sweden. In those vast polar lands, the heat is coming to an end and the mosquitoes are gorging themselves with blood before a rapidly approaching death.

Here, lingering of high summer.
Still I want to sing
maturity of life,

---

16. Brother Michel (Bergmann 1936–2009), born of German missionary parents in New Guinea, went to secondary school in Australia and then studied sociology in France and Germany. He spent most of his community life in Brazil as the brother responsible for the *fraternité* there. He died on a visit to Australia as a result of a freak accident while swimming in the ocean.

the swollen fruit of the chestnut tree,
the splendor of the mild night,
the scent of leaves too soon fallen,
grass drenched with a heavy dew,
soil's thirst quenched.

September 7, 1971

The day before yesterday, Grégoire[17] and Jean-François[18] returned from Sotto il Monte accompanied by Giuseppe Roncalli. In his old age, he looks so much like his brother, Pope John XXIII. Fulgenzio, his grandson, is here too. I had already noticed his solid maturity last year. He is only twenty.

Giuseppe Roncalli speaks of his childhood, that of John XXIII. Their elderly uncle owned a total of seven books and spoke to them about the gospel. Winter and summer alike, all went to Mass at 5:30 every morning. In the evening, the family would pray together.

When he was papal nuncio, the future John XXIII used to help out his family. They had only a few cows and one day one of them died. He wrote them, "The money I am sending is for sugar and oil. I can do no more. I bless the cows, even the one that died."

Then Giuseppe Roncalli spoke of his first visit to his brother, once he was pope. The two brothers discussed how certain Christians live in great wealth. The pope says, "I remind them: look at what happens in the Gospel to those who are rich." Like the old peasant from Bergamo that he is, Giuseppe Roncalli often alludes to the god Mammon—money. He notes that the young people stay here on our hill in poor living conditions and tells Fulgenzio, "From here will arise something that my brother began."

---

17. Brother Grégoire (Gérard Huni, 1933–1997), from a French and Swiss family. He spent many years in Africa, in the *fraternités* of brothers in Algeria, Rwanda, Kenya, and Senegal.

18. Brother Jean-François (Hans Oechsli, 1935–2000), originally from German-speaking Switzerland, is remembered among other things for his beautiful singing voice.

September 8, 1971

One question has kept coming up this summer: "How are we to continue once we have left Taizé?" And I would reply: Nobody can possibly grasp all that there is in the gospel. But if during your stay here you have understood just one word, just one act—almost nothing—then put into practice that word, that act, at once and intensively. When you have put one foot forward, that step will lead you on to other steps. Live out the little we have understood, and create on the basis of that tiny intuition, on the basis of our own poverty. Strive to find one intuition and to live by it.

September 29, 1971

A question from Jacqueline: "How are we to reconcile inner silence and contemplation with being politically involved alongside movements which see violence as a means of action?"

September 30, 1971

I said to a visitor from Argentina: as I listen to so many young political activists, it is mainly the left ear that is at work, but the right ear is not completely idle either!

October 1, 1971

Certain mental structures formed in childhood remain for ever, and around them all the events of life weave and reweave themselves.

A memory comes back to mind. When I was about eight, I brought down from the attic all the best-bound volumes, including Diderot's *Encyclopedia*. My mother was not very happy to see me organizing a whole library of old, dusty books in my room. But my father told her, "Let him be; a happy childhood marks a whole life."

1971

October 2, 1971

Bicycle ride with Robert. Both of us were surprised on discovering, ten minutes away from the house, the river Grosne at peace, snaking between oak trees. We continued on foot as far as the bridge of Cortemblin. On our left, a red sun was dipping into far-off mist, on our right a great moon already high in the heavens. The unfamiliar meanderings of the Grosne propelled us in every direction. All my life I have longed for that landscape; there it was at our door and I had not realized it.

October 6, 1971

Today I have nothing else to write but this: if so much suffering is for Christ, for his body the church, and for humankind, then I will continue.

October 15, 1971

This morning, something unique. In one long line, all the Carmelite sisters from Chalon were present at our prayer. They were leaving for good the convent where their community had been living for the past three centuries and were on their way to their new home not far from us. At the end of the prayer, I gave them a few hazelnuts and told them:

"These nuts were brought from Avila this spring and they come from a tree that tradition says was planted by St. Theresa. Tradition and poetry join hands. Tradition weaves a tapestry that expresses continuity with numerous and varied threads—some dark and some bright. As long as it does not become rigid, the fabric it creates can go on developing indefinitely, always covered with new designs."

October 16, 1971

Mrs. Gandhi[19] replies in a rather frustrating way: "It is kind of you to offer to send volunteers to work in the refugee camps. But I feel they can contribute more by mobilizing public opinion in their own countries."

Always the same refusal of the North by the South. Make those around you more aware. We are in complete agreement, even if it takes us a long way, even to prison, as one of my brothers was saying. But communion cannot just be limited to that.

October 19, 1971

Visited Francisco this morning.[20] Always the same pale, emaciated face. He is afraid that he is not getting any better. The oldest of his children, Martinho, stands near his bed. His wife is close by, with another child in her arms. Through the window I can see young people coming and going on the open space near the bells. They never suspect that in the same house that they come to on arriving, upstairs, there is a young couple of Portuguese emigrants with many burdens to bear.

October 21, 1971

For weeks now, every morning I have opened the curtains with the same thrill. A warm light bounds from the ground in crystal greys. Beneath the lime trees and the maples is a carpet of leaves. From time to time a slight mist rises from the valley and fills the sky, then these layers of leaves begin to sparkle.

October 22, 1971

Letter from a young man, from the heart of Africa:

19. Indira Gandhi (1917–1984), prime minister of India.
20. See entry for June 27, 1971, p. 105.

"Yesterday I saw a friend I have known since January. I first met him on the road, uneducated and impoverished. Afterwards he came to see me. He was looking for work. Now he often comes and tells me about his family and friends. I have done nothing for him except listen to what he says. When I told him the other day that I would soon have to return to France, he spoke these words: 'I was a man with nothing; I did not have life. You listened to me. You gave me life and God. In Europe everyone is rich; there you will have no poor people to befriend.'"

October 26, 1971

Some people underrate themselves; others push themselves forward. Both attitudes come from the same narcissism, that regression into childishness that keeps us from being ourselves.

October 30, 1971

Since last evening I have been meeting with Eugene Carson Blake,[21] the secretary general of the World Council of Churches. Towards the end of our conversation he affirms: "All my life I have been involved in running church institutions. I have always known what had to be said or done. In today's situation, I do not know any more." I ask him, "Can I repeat to the young people in the church this evening what you have just said?" He agrees. But I shall add this: it is when we are in a desert that we can expect a prophetic word.

November 8, 1971

Hesitated greatly whether to go to Paris in response to an invitation from Mrs. Gandhi. I found it better for a brother to go with

---

21. Eugene Carson Blake (1906–1985), pastor in the Presbyterian Church of the United States, secretary general of the World Council of Churches in Geneva from 1966 to 1972. A close friend of Brother Roger and the community.

a message. That is not my place. Why? I find it hard to explain it to myself exactly . . . traces of puritanism . . . feeling ill-at-ease in the presence of those with political responsibilities . . . and yet this woman, in the present drama of Bangladesh, inspires sympathy.[22]

November 10, 1971

Often, especially since the announcement of the Council of Youth, I have heard how certain priests or ministers experience a sense of frustration on seeing so many young people coming to the hill here, while their churches are emptying. Occasionally their pain turns into bitterness. Some even go so far as to publish articles to misrepresent the young who gather here and the life they live when they are together. I have just been talking with one such person here in my room. . . .

November 13, 1971

Long interview for Canadian television. The cameraman, already aging, has been here before; between us there exists a kind of complicity. The reporter, mistrustful of the church without being aggressive, asks relevant and honest questions. I give replies I had not intended to give:

All of us in the West have inherited a mentality marked by the legalism and imperialism of ancient Rome, even though we may consider ourselves free of them. The churches of the Reformation believed that they were ridding themselves of legalism and have simply produced a new kind. Certain Marxist countries denounce imperialism and organize another form of it, just as effective.

Should we employ a great deal of energy to change the structures of the church? If that is simply in order to create new ones, what is the point? There are other ways forward.

22. After several months of a bitter war of independence, East Bengal, supported in December 1971 by a decisive intervention from India and its prime minister Indira Gandhi, managed to separate itself from the western part of Pakistan and become Bangladesh.

1971

November 15, 1971

Spent an hour in Daniel's pottery. I enter with the attentiveness one always brings to places consecrated by ardent workmanship.

On a blackboard: figures, diagrams, mathematical equations. Hooked onto a plank are little colored plaques, specimens of glaze with a formula written above each.

Systematic research leading to the creation of glazes based on minerals or plants found locally, using ashes from straw, reeds, ferns, acacia and oak trees. . . . Lengthy preparation before even beginning to work on the lump of clay. A whole series of processes before each object is entrusted to the glow of the flames, finally to emerge sparkling and fascinating by its form.

We talk together. I have the impression that I surprise Daniel when I say: spontaneously I find old people and children set me most at my ease. If I have come to be so attentive to the young, that may be because I have heard so many of them tell me of the fog they are passing through.

November 17, 1971

More and more I find myself telling young men and women about to leave here for their homes far away: in female monastic communities there are women practiced in the exercise of discernment, often as a result of many years of experience. Go and seek, in dialogue with one of them, to be understood just as you are.

In times past, in communities of men, when it was recognized that some had a charism, a great capacity for listening and intuition, they were called to communicate the freedom of forgiveness, whether they were priests or laymen (in Eastern Orthodoxy, the *starets*).

The same gifts exist in certain women living in community. Why has a similar feminine vocation of listening and intuition to convey liberation never been recognized?

November 24, 1971

Heading towards Rome in the train, I realize that the most intense hours of these past few days were not those that I thought, the two evening meetings in churches packed with young people at Turin and Bologna.

What mattered most was this morning's encounter with some theology students. I studied their faces and in some I could sense skepticism, although accompanied by the desire to give their whole lives. We live in a civilization of criticism, but criticism supposes education and self-knowledge, otherwise it is nothing more than a constant projection of one's own inner devastation on others, on the People of God.

November 26, 1971

We have been in Rome for two days now. After so many stays here, I can measure the long distance covered, more often arduous than easy. Why have I been so determined to persevere, when everything encouraged me to stay at Taizé? Why have I been so convinced of the necessity of these conversations here in Rome? I have been compelled to continue them, irresistibly, as though moved by a force coming from beyond myself.

November 28, 1971

First Sunday in Advent. There is a sea air blowing over the city. Yesterday, we walked until our legs were stiff. Today too, I was intending to walk but some young people recognized us in the street, so we had to start inviting them to the house.

For several hours past, a breeze has been blowing through the open window into my room. That is no substitute for the beam of sunlight which, at Taizé, shines on the wide wooden planks of the floor. Here my room, opening on to the courtyard, is in perpetual twilight.

1971

November 30, 1971

Coming home this evening with Max, we entered the courtyard of the Villa Laetitia Bonaparte for a second and walked to the far end, to look out on the crisscrossing lights of the passing cars. A confused hubbub reaches us at the back of the courtyard and, through the high gateway, Piazza Venezia advances, recoils, dances.

December 3, 1971

Long private conversation with Pope Paul VI. The mystic in him prevails. He longs to grasp the plan of God. When I talk to him of the young, he understands so well. Never a word of warning from his lips.

At the close of the conversation, I say words I had not intended to speak: "The name of Taizé is heavy for us to bear; there are days when I long to see it vanish." "No," the pope replies, "the name of Taizé cannot disappear." And he makes a generous parallel with another historical example.[23] Paul VI goes on to add, "The first time that we met, you told me that you were pilgrims on the move and I have always remembered that." That must have been when we spoke together in 1949. True, we are pilgrims, our means are poor. And the pope concludes, "I too am poor."

December 8, 1971

Walk through the old medieval streets. Inner courtyards beckon, hidden at the end of rundown alleys. We enter one of them. A fountain is trickling into an Etruscan coffin. A wall carpeted with greenery. Great pots overflowing with camellias. Above our heads, hanging galleries held up by goodness knows what, since all is so decrepit. Washing hung in the windows.

Reaching the Via Giulia, we glimpse a green garden through an open gate. We enter briskly and find a mandarin grove, set

---

23. Brother Roger was impressed at hearing the pope compare Taizé to Assisi.

against the hills rising beyond the Tiber. In the depth of European winter, two girls are picking an abundant crop.

December 11, 1971

The texts of the recent synod have just been made public. At the end of a long day, I have addressed a message to Paul VI to tell him especially:

"Celibacy, folly of the Gospel in human eyes and proclamation of the coming Kingdom, will stimulate the church of God in its unique vocation to be the salt of the earth. Celibacy is certainly not an easy option; it is a way by which men and women give their whole lives to Christ without keeping back part for the future. Because of it they receive a hundredfold, but with persecutions, experienced as an inner struggle for those entrusted to them by God. Far from contradicting the holiness of Christian marriage, celibacy will encourage Christians to discover the specific vocation of the laity—a 'royal priesthood' given to each Christian, which involves living Christ for others. Thus Christians will bear more explicitly in themselves a share in the common ministry of the church."[24]

---

24. Following the Second Vatican Council, Pope Paul VI instituted a synod of bishops. From September 30 to November 6, 1971, the second ordinary synodal assembly was held. It had a twofold theme: "The ministerial priesthood and justice in the world." Regarding the priesthood, the bishops asked the question of ordaining married men and gave a restrictive answer out of fear of calling priestly celibacy into question. When the texts were made public, Brother Roger, who had seen the pope's deep concern a few days earlier, decided spontaneously on his own initiative to send him a personal message of encouragement. He did not imagine that Paul VI would be very touched and wish to publish the message in *l'Osservatore Romano*. In agreeing for it to be published, Brother Roger never dreamed that it would spark a controversy in certain French Protestant circles.

December 12, 1971

Without at all watering down the force of the call to celibacy, yesterday's synodal text does not exclude the possibility that the priesthood may be conferred on married men.

In recent months, I was unable to reconcile myself to the idea that the synod might abolish completely the link between priesthood and celibacy. I prepared myself to consent. But there were days when the depth of my concern was in direct proportion to the question: does the Catholic Church realize the radical reversal of values inherent in such a change? Priestly celibacy, folly of the gospel, has maintained in the heart of the church a mystical vein: the church has been led towards the invisible, the mystery of Christ, the irrational element of the gospel. The marriage of priests would be a move towards the simply functional, the instrumental.

That there is a need, in certain local situations, to ordain married men is something I am convinced of. But it is important that such men should first have proved themselves in married life, so as to avoid a future crisis in their ministry with their children in disagreement or in open revolt, or because their life's partner is unable to continue living confined in an ecclesiastical setup.

The marriage of priests will not resolve anything of the present crisis, which has nothing to do with marriage or celibacy. The collapse in the number of vocations is just as great in Protestant theological faculties, whose students have always been free to marry. As for the lack of emotional maturity, that is something existing both in single people and in those who are married.

The brutal and accelerating decline in vocations has its cause elsewhere, and calls for infinitely more basic transformations.

December 13, 1971

Have been continuing yesterday's reflection about the priesthood and the laity.

As far as the priesthood is concerned, although it may mean having few priests, it is important to change completely the way of preparing men for the ministry. Their preparation should inculcate an ability to ask questions about one's existence one's whole life long—to discover the why, and then the why of the why, of one's behavior. Studies which are more a kind of birth process than an accumulation of book knowledge. In the future, knowledge will be acquired more and more in successive stages, all through life. The main thing is to achieve the permeability that will enable someone to assimilate the rapid succession of waves which will pass through the human mind. All of this is true as well for schools and universities in general.

As for the laity, how to enable Christians to discover the share of the common ministry entrusted to each one? Faced with a lack of priests, laypeople will be obliged to take their part—immense and almost unexplored—in a ministry that until now has been exercised almost solely by the clergy. The result will be a new complementarity between laypeople and priests.

December 22, 1971

Return to Taizé. I am obliged to recognize the use to which my message to Paul VI has been put. A few sentences of it were published in the French press. Based on this, a denominational press agency published a commentary without quoting the terms I actually used, which distorts the sense of the text. Should I in turn reply in the press? No. All my life, when I have been attacked, I have striven within myself to maintain silence.

December 23, 1971

This evening I read a letter from a young couple. Knowing their positions, I expected to find them writing reproachfully about the message to Paul VI, which has earned me so many letters of protest. But instead, they announce the birth of a child. . . .

December 26, 1971

Some young women tell me that their attempt to live together in community has not been successful.

Success is a social notion that is poles apart from the gospel. To aim to succeed begets a subtle form of self-centeredness. Accept that we always stumble. Our expressions are awkward, never perfect. Our symbols are ambiguous.

December 27, 1971

The ecumenical movement at present sets us on the horns of a dilemma: how can we enter into a more universal communion without asking anyone to deny the faith transmitted to them in all honesty by their ancestors? As a temporary solution, for the generation of the present transitional period, can we accept the possibility of a "double allegiance"?[25]

December 31, 1971

In the sky a few pale stars, deep night and hard frost.

Once again, I have closed the door on the silence of my room. I have loved too much with my whole being for solitude to become a matter of course.

Age gains ground little by little. To everything consent is given. The years have checked the turbulent tide. At last I know how to love. Within me, the inexhaustible rivers of love that spring up at every moment flow peaceably between banks rising in the midst of sweeping plains. No trace of bitterness. Not that the fire

---

25. A month later, during the week of prayer for Christian unity in January 1972, Brother Roger suggested publicly this possibility of a "double allegiance." In the face of the oppositions that this idea aroused, both on the Protestant and the Catholic side, he gave it up after three months and began searching for another way to formulate a road towards reconciliation. He would explain later that he had launched this proposal as a trial balloon.

is extinguished. It will keep burning on and on, until the chill of death.

At present nothing appalls me, neither life nor death. Expectation of unending rest for the flesh and blood. . . . So then, one winter's night, may that gentle rest come and with it the life that has no end.

1972

The early months of 1972 continue along the same lines as the previous year. Aside from a brief visit to Catalonia, Brother Roger remained in Taizé, in a life made up of encounters with brothers and friends, sometimes by letter, reflections on faith and on the situation of the church, culminating in the Holy Week and Easter celebrations with thousands of young people on the hill, during which a new stage of the preparation of the Council of Youth was announced.

January 5, 1972

Resume this journal. Nothing can replace writing, the unhurried reflecting, worked out on the shining paper, under the lamp, in rounded characters.

January 7, 1972

In days which are darkened by the discovery of such somber realities as repressive intolerance, I like to remember John XXIII saying, "Be joyful, seek the best and let the sparrows chirp."[1]

It is two in the morning, In the garden, the mildness of a spring night. Sat for a few minutes out on the porch, from where I could see through the window into the *salle claire*. Its pine floor was warm with tints of lemon.

January 14, 1972

Yesterday, I asked little Jean-Paul for whom we should pray: "For the people of the whole world."

So strong a sense of the universal in such a young child! True, for two thousand years now we have been singing our inconceivable hope in a Christ come to set every human being free—not only those who explicitly draw their life from him, but every person everywhere, not just a few privileged people or a single ethnic group, but members of every race and people.

January 20, 1972

At times, people of my generation find themselves caught between the jaws of a vise, between explanations required by the old, weary

---

1. In reality, the pope himself was quoting a phrase of Don Bosco's: "The best thing we can do in this world is to be joyful, do good and let the sparrows chirp."

church and the aspirations of the rising generations. Do not turn your back on either of them.

January 22, 1972

A letter in the mail that counts. It is from a peasant woman. I am going to copy it here. When I come to choose passages from this journal to publish, I wonder if I shall dare to include these lines?

"I am making a fool of myself by writing to you. Who am I, a poor countrywoman, to write to Brother Roger? All the same, I want to say thank you . . . especially for *Festival without End*. In that book, a friend is talking to me of a Friend in words I feel but cannot express. Thank you for your optimism, your confidence in humanity. And for the poetry, so youthful and fresh in spite of all the difficulties."

I quickly reply to say that both of us are cut from the same cloth.

February 10, 1972

Went walking with Clement[2] in the vineyards at Saules. Red soil. Vast horizons ending, above the Jura, in a long bank of fog. Such outings are refreshing. This brother, with his joy at being alive, his peals of laughter. . . .

February 16, 1972

With Christians split into countless denominations, it is easy to keep finding new reasons for remaining on parallel tracks which, by definition, will never come together. But these reasons become a way of avoiding the issue. In the end, will this not betray the ecumenical longing of the People of God?

---

2. Brother Clement (Laurent Laufer, 1936–2004), from French-speaking Switzerland.

February 18, 1972

Having had Catholic brothers for several years now and forming with them in our house a single community has allowed us to discover this creative way forward: begin first by living together, and then a common faithfulness does not take long to grow.

February 19, 1972

A long letter from Hector.[3] The struggle in which he is involved with poor peasants in Colombia is a hard one. Having too many things to do this morning, I left part of his letter to read during the afternoon. There, he tells me that Bishop Valencia has been killed in an accident. This man of great openness, misunderstood by many, was a point of reference for many young Colombian Christians and even for some non-Christian revolutionaries.

After prayer this evening, we were together to welcome a new brother into the community. I would have liked to have spoken of this bishop's death. Who is going to fill the void left in the lives of so many young Colombians fighting for greater justice? That question affected me so deeply that I lost my voice. Impossible to utter three words. I had to cut short our council.

February 20, 1972

Yesterday my mother was saying to a friend, "I talk to God; we understand each other well. I pray for everybody. On days when I am too weak for that, God understands too." A few days ago she said to Ghislain, "What counts for God is the heart."

February 27, 1972

Arrived yesterday at Barcelona, invited by the abbot of Montserrat, who was in Taizé last year. On Friday, passing through Perpignan,

---

3. See p. 43, note 37.

1972

I was eager to make the acquaintance of Madame Durocher, the grandmother of one of my young brothers.

As night was falling, we found the narrow street where she lives. I spot a woman with white hair arranged in a bun; in her features I recognize her grandson, and so I embrace her spontaneously, in the middle of the street!

We enter a small dark room. Out of breath from climbing the stairs, she gradually recovers her voice and it becomes melodious. She announces that the pastor of their parish, and the bishop, want to come to say hello to me. I try to resist. I am here for her, to hear what she has to say. The little I have already grasped suggests how great a quality of intuition lies within her.

Here on the second floor I glimpse, in the gloom, a terrace. Greenery at this height? She leads me out onto it. "Here is where I spend the summer." The palm tree at the center of this tiny garden is the highest in the town. There are flower beds nestling in thick foliage. I breathe in the perfume of this tiny piece of land at the heart of an old city. In a flash I imagine her, all through the summer, hidden here—fulfillment in solitude.

After the meal she talks about her husband. One image follows another. One Christmas, in Provence at the end of the war, they had almost nothing to eat. In spite of her husband's reticence, she went and bought a kilo of sugar on the black market to make some sweets. The words weave together, mistletoe and pale honey . . .

It is getting late. In spite of protests, Robert, Patrick, and I continue our journey, and only stop to sleep once we have crossed the Spanish border.

February 28, 1972

Yesterday we were walking along a path with a view of the buildings of Monserrat perched between two steep peaks.

Our Christian life is also set between two mountains! There is the mount of the transfiguration, where Christ makes use of all that is in us and transforms it—both the good and the not-so-good, hatred and love—and the mount on which Jesus knew temptation.

So attractive, the one who there offered him domination over all the kingdoms of the earth. . . .

March 4, 1972

I have pinned to my wall a photograph of Zhou Enlai, cut out of a Spanish newspaper. The statesman is lifting his hand in farewell as Nixon is about to leave China. On the face of this aging intellectual, a suffering too deep for words.

March 18, 1972

Pierre-Yves[4] was speaking of that voice that doubts and mutters within us: "Oh yes, God chooses this or that person, but I have nothing to make him consider me; my prayer is nothing more than a projection of myself." And Pierre-Yves then made his comment: is that really humility? It almost is, and yet it is just the opposite. It is simply a form of exaggerated self-love, a love turned into hatred. In fact, self-hate is closer to pride than to humility. If we refuse to believe, even just a little, in our love for God, we shall be unable to believe in God's love for us.

March 23, 1972

If at present, all over the world, certain Christian institutions are falling to pieces, is that not, in the end, all to the good for the churches . . . perhaps with a view to a communion?

---

4. Brother Pierre-Yves (Emery, 1929–2023), from French-speaking Switzerland. Wrote several works of theology and later devoted himself to translating Bernard of Clairvaux and other Cistercian monks from the Middle Ages. Often made visits to other monasteries and sometimes gave talks and retreats to the monks and nuns.

March 24, 1972

A young couple from Argentina inform me that they have decided to live in community with other couples. I ask them if they are willing to agree for such a project to remain provisional. I know that any family, no matter how open and generous the parents may be, is bound to condition its members. But is their plan not going to submit their children to too many pressures?

We are asking the same questions with several couples who are thinking of coming to live near us on the hill.

March 25, 1972

A few months ago we learned that, unbeknownst to us, a group of capitalists had formed a company with the aim of setting up a luxury hotel, a motel and a holiday village not far from Taizé. Certain businessmen had been persuaded that this was an opportunity not to be missed. Relief on learning that their plans have misfired.

March 26, 1972

Dreamed last night in poetry. I am a child, together with my sisters. On a bright morning, we are climbing along a wide lane covered by high, thick greenery. In the foliage brightly colored birds are flitting. A splendid green bird with gleaming plumage comes swooping down beside me. As we reach the top of the hill, the horizon opens onto wide expanses of uncultivated countryside. On the road is a shop. We stop. I fill a wicker basket with all kinds of things, toys and other presents.

March 27, 1972

Monday in Holy Week. The readings of the passion fall into ground stirred up by recent events. With many young people, here and far away, we have allowed the desert soil of our beings to be plowed over. Many have met together, in the farthest corners of the earth. So many discoveries, a wealth of friendship and mutual trust.

But shadows, too, have been discovered. In recent months we have had to submit to almost unbearable pressures. We have found that there exists a visceral fear of the young. And the fear that here we pay far too much attention to them. How often have I heard people say, "Those young people are going to wrap you around their little finger!"

No real adventure can be undertaken together without temptation appearing. The tempter offered Christ all the kingdoms of the world if he would only submit to him. Those kingdoms have names: the quite illusory attempt to gain influence over others, the desire for power. And that inevitably leads to everything drying up.

If we ignore these rear-guard combats, what remains is a great dynamism that can take us far, very far.

March 28, 1972

In all the current changes in human behavior there is one constant: the need to live in the here and now, which means a lack of interest in history. Yet we are always linked to a past, recent or distant, that no severance can ever really obliterate. Ancestral memory? Genetic memory? Who can decide?

April 2, 1972

Easter morning. After the Eucharist, the crowds coming to give me the Easter greeting were so great that I had to laugh to myself at my limits. I found a gesture: I would lay on my shoulder for a second the head of each person as they passed in an unbroken stream. Some would say a few words, sometimes something quite serious. In two hours, so many faces!

April 3, 1972

Too dazzling to be seen, God is a God who blinds our sight. It is Christ who channels this consuming fire and allows God to shine through without dazzling us.

Christ is present, close to each one, whether we know him or not. He is there in secret, a light in our darkness, a fire burning in our heart. He is so bound up with us that he lives within us, even when we are unaware of him.

But Christ is also, as God, someone other than ourselves. He exists in himself; he could exist without us. He is in front of us as the object of our tireless search in a face-to-face relationship. He stands ahead of the human person, beyond us.

The day will come when, in him, all created worlds will find fulfillment, worlds perhaps inhabited by other creatures made in the image of God. If, beyond our present perceptions, a new dimension of communion were to be discovered, its source would still unfailingly be in this same Christ. The Body of Christ, his church, can only widen more and more to the dimensions of the whole universe.

April 4, 1972

Of all that has happened in the past few days, what was the most compelling? Of course, sixteen thousand young people here together. Of course, the announcement that the Council of Youth will begin in 1974. But above all the prayer together. During these Easter days, it has carried everything, like a ship making its way through a foaming sea. It has borne us forward in spite of the burden of tensions and struggles, whether caused by present obstacles or ones lying ahead. Creating as free human beings, we know what we are searching for. We have nothing to fear.

SELECT BIBLIOGRAPHY

Writings by Brother Roger

Fidanzio, Marcello, ed. *Brother Roger of Taizé: Essential Writings.* Maryknoll, NY: Orbis, 2006.
Anthology with biographical introduction.

Dynamic of the Provisional. London: Mowbray, 1981.

Glimmers of Happiness. Chicago: GIA, 2007.
Brother Roger reflects on events and people that influenced his life and calling.

God is Love Alone. Chicago: GIA, 2003.
The essentials of Brother Roger's thinking and personal accounts from the story of Taizé.

Peace of Heart in All Things. Chicago: GIA, 2004.
A brief meditation for each day of the year.

The Rule of Taizé. London: SPCK, 2013.
The original text expressing the fundamentals of the life of the Taizé Community.

Books about Taizé

Clément, Olivier. *Taizé: A Meaning to Life.* Chicago: GIA, 1997.
Santos, Jason Brian. *A Community Called Taizé: A Story of Prayer, Worship and Reconciliation.* Downers Grove, IL: IVP, 2008.
Spink, Kathryn. *A Universal Heart: The Life and Vision of Brother Roger of Taizé.* Chicago: GIA, 1986, 2005.

SELECT BIBLIOGRAPHY

DVDs (available at www.giamusic.com)

Moments in the Life of Brother Roger
Meeting Brother Roger of Taizé

www.taize.fr

Information in twenty-eight languages about the community, meetings at Taizé and elsewhere (online registration), suggestions for prayer, the songs of Taizé, etc.

Subject Index

Africa, 48, 49, 76, 78, 101–2, 108, 116–17
Alain, Brother, 49, 95
Aldrin, Buzz, 29
Athenagoras, Patriarch of Constantinople, 57
Ameugny, 74
authority, 23, 52

Balzac, Honoré de, 76
Beatrice, 103–5
Benedictines, 24
Besançon, 16
Blake, Eugene Carson, 117
Boegner, Marc, 90
Braillard, Marie, 22
Brazil, 49, 106–7, 110, 112
Bruno, Brother, 85
Buisson, Marcel, 100
Bultmann, Rudolf, 33

Camara, Dom Helder, 66–67
Cano, Pablo, 28
Cano, Pedro, 56
Carmelites, 115
Catholicism, 4–5, 16, 17, 23, 26, 130
celibacy, 70, 108, 122, 123
Chapelle-sur-Oron, 22
Charles-Eugène, Brother, 85
Chicago, 15
China, 106, 109, 132

Church of Reconciliation, 34, 97
Clement, Brother, 129
Cluny, 53, 72
communities, small Christian, 31, 34, 95, 125, 133
cooperative farm (COPEX), 11
Cormatin, 9
council of the community, 81
Council of Youth, 18, 51, 54, 58–59, 62, 64, 65, 90, 99, 102, 111, 118, 135
Crema, 18–19
Culles-les-Roches, 100

dance, 35–36
Daniel (de Montmollin), Brother, 89, 119
death, 43, 47, 50, 60, 96, 125–26
Denis, Brother, 101
divisions among Christians, 4–5, 50, 69, 125, 129

Eboli, 85–88
ecumenism, *see* divisions among Christians
Estavayer, 16
eucharist, 8, 16, 19, 29, 32–33, 57, 98

faithfulness, 14, 29, 34, 54, 63
Fatima, 9–10

Fernandes, Dom Luis Gonzaga, 106–7, 110
Foucauld, Charles de, 62
Franco, Francisco, 90
fraternities of brothers, 15, 46, 102
freedom, 70

Gandhi, Indira, 116, 117
Gafaringa, Edouard, 101–2
Germany, 3, 17, 23
Ghislain, Brother, 43, 130
Gilberte de Rougemont, Sister, 97–98
Grégoire, Brother, 113

Hitler, Adolf, 23

Irenaeus of Lyons, Saint, 78
Italy, 18–20, 29, 37–42, 47, 50, 53–54, 72, 82, 85–89, 94, 120–24

Japan, 102
Jean-François, Brother, 113
John XXIII, Pope, 20, 38, 113, 128
José, Brother, 98
Kaburungu, Stanislas, 76, 78, 108
Kennedy, Robert, 4
Latin America, 6, 25, 33, 39, 40, 41, 49, 64, 70–71, 75, 76, 77, 82, 84, 106–7, 110, 114, 130, 133
Lebrun, Lucien-Sidroine (former bishop of Autun), 61
Little Brothers of Jesus, 62
liturgy, 18, 19, 56
Lord's Supper. *See* eucharist.

Macon, 22, 36–37, 42, 97
Marc, Brother, 47
Marguerite de Beaumont, Sister, 97–98
Mary, mother of Jesus, 9–10, 46, 80, 84, 98
Manziana, Carlo, 18–19
Martí, José, 65

Max (Thurian), Brother, 56, 74, 121
Maximinio, 58–59
Michel, Brother, 112
Montceau-les-Mines, 99
Montserrat, 130, 131
Mounier, Emmanuel, 72

New York, 103–4
Northern Ireland, 109–110
nonbelievers, 66, 85

Oliver, Raymond, 80
Olivier, Brother, 27

Paris, 8–9, 51, 90
Patrick, Brother, 22, 131
Paul VI, Pope, 42, 61–62, 89, 121, 122, 124
Perpignan, 130–31
Peter, Saint, 27
Philippe, Brother, 57
Pierre-Yves, Brother, 132
Portugal, 9–10, 67, 74, 79, 105–6, 107–8, 116
prayer, 3, 8, 12, 27, 35, 63
protest, 5, 6, 17, 25–26, 60–61
Protestantism, 4–5, 23, 69
Rasiwala, Moiz, 51
Recife (Brazil), 112
reconciliation, 32–33, 65
Reynold, Brother, 35
Robert, Brother, 64, 115, 131
Rome, 37–42, 85, 88–89, 120–24
Roncalli, Giuseppe, 113
Roncalli, Zaverio, 20
Roosevelt, Madame, 35–36
Rutishauser, Peter, 96

Saint Benoit-sur-Loire, 24
Saone River, 36
Schutz-Marsauche, Amelie (Brother Roger's mother), 32, 81, 130
Schutz, Charles (Brother Roger's father), 50

Schutz, Genevieve (Brother Roger's sister), 24, 37, 88
Schutz, Lily (Brother Roger's sister), 76
Schutz, Yvonne (Brother Roger's sister), 49
Second Vatican Council, *see* Vatican Council II
silence, 2
Sotto-il-Monte, 20, 113
Spain, 55–56, 90, 95, 100
St. Gengoux-le-National, 72, 101
suffering, 11, 32
Switzerland, 22, 59

Teresa of Avila, Saint, 59, 115
thanksgiving, 43
Thomas, Brother, 88
Thurian, André, 96
Tolstoy, Leo, 83

Tomkins, Oliver, 97
Torres, Hector, 43, 130
Toulouse, 99

Unamuno, Miguel de, 65
United States, 103–4

Vatican, 40, 89, 108–9
Vatican Council II, 4–5, 122
violence, 32, 55, 71, 94
Vivien, Jean, 21
Voillaume, René, 62

World Council of Churches, 59

young people, 2, 25, 29, 30, 31, 32, 46, 60, 66, 73, 88

Zhou Enlai, 132